"Sibling relationships are the lon_
rarely studied. Johanna Dobrich ;
and artfully explores this life ꞯ _
work. In *Survivor Siblings*, she examines the experience of ambiguous
loss embedded in these sibling relations. (For me, it was my little
brother's polio.) Johanna Dobrich has wisely uncovered a critical sibling
experience that some of us have had, but she is the first scholar I know of
who is looking into it. Bravo! We need to know ourselves before we can
help others to know themselves."

Dr. Pauline Boss, Author of *Ambiguous Loss*, 2000, Harvard University
Press, 2000; *Loss, Trauma and Resilience*, 2006, WW Norton

"With a soulful, fierce intellect and unflinching honesty, Johanna Dobrich
brings her reader into an intimate and keenly observed examination of
the ways in which her experience as the sibling of a severely disabled
brother has shaped both her psychic life and analytic understanding.
In doing so, she creates a larger portal for considering how minds
respond to developmental traumas that go unseen, unacknowledged and
unformulated. This impressive book joins memoir and interview material
with a rigorous engagement of contemporary relational thinking. The
result is a richly textured tapestry that marries experience with theory to
produce an inspiring clinical wisdom that demonstrates how healing the
other and healing oneself is a false distinction. Whether or not you are a
survivor sibling or even a sibling, you will find yourself in these pages and
know yourself and analytic theory all the better for it."

Martin Stephen Frommer, PhD, Faculty,
Stephen Mitchell Relational Study Center
Associate Editor, *Psychoanalytic Dialogues*

"This long-overdue book belongs in the library of all psychoanalytic
therapists. It is a significant contribution to relational scholarship. It is
also a gift to the many therapists who grew up alongside a damaged
brother or sister, chose their profession partly because of their struggles
and achievements as a sibling, and yet have never been fully able to tell
their complex stories – partly because psychoanalysis itself lacked the
space for such narratives. Dobrich has mined her own experience as a
'survivor sibling' in a ground-breaking qualitative study. Her voice is
intimate and compassionate, her interviews with colleagues of comparable

backgrounds are riveting, and the illumination she offers to readers of any sibling background is profound."

Nancy McWilliams, PhD, ABPP, Rutgers Graduate
School of Applied and Professional Psychology

"As a "survivor sibling" myself, I am deeply moved both by Johanna Dobrich's description of her own experience as the sibling of a seriously disabled brother and by the insights she has drawn from 15 deeply intimate interviews with other analysts, all of whom are fellow survivor siblings. Dobrich clearly portrays the pervasive impact on family life of the presence of a special needs child. Not only are the needs of normally functioning children eclipsed in this family environment, but their sacrifice is typically unacknowledged by parents, who are themselves struggling for emotional survival. This demand for self-sacrifice, combined with "interpersonal silence" within the family, can make it very difficult for a survivor sibling to develop a separate sense of self. Dobrich does a wonderful job of drawing our attention, as analysts, to this emotional dilemma and to the extra importance of sibling relationships in any family history that has included co-existence with a disabled child."

Sue Bloland, PhD, Author of *In The Shadow of Fame: A Memoir By The Daughter of Erik H. Erikson* (2005, Viking Publishers)

"In Johanna Dobrich's *Working with Survivor Siblings in Psychoanalysis: Ability and Disability in Clinical Process*, we have a major and long-awaited new contribution that fills a tremendous gap in the fields of psychoanalysis. Lacking in all these different traditions is a sustained, coherent, and comprehensive account of what happens to a human subject, personally, relationally, and professionally, when she lives alongside and survives a disabled sibling. Beyond sublimation as de-instinctualization, what is her call when she herself becomes a Relational psychoanalyst? Dobrich provides a multitude of rich naïve descriptions from her research that are themselves a platform for thinking about difficulties in mentalization, microtraumatic attachments, identifications, and uncanny reactivations of maladaptive attachments across generations that a patient can resubjectivize in a clinical relationship. This book is timely, supremely relevant and a pleasure to read."

Maurice Apprey, Professor of Psychiatry, Member of the Academy
of Distinguished Educators, University of Virginia School of
Medicine, is a training and supervising analyst of
the Contemporary Freudian Society

Working with Survivor Siblings in Psychoanalysis

Working with Survivor Siblings in Psychoanalysis: Ability and Disability in Clinical Process explores a previously neglected area in the field of psychoanalysis, addressing undertheorized concepts on siblings, disabilities, and psychic survivorship, and broadening our conceptualization of the enduring effects of lateral relations on human development.

What happens to a person's sense of self both personally and professionally when they grow up alongside a severely disabled sibling? Through a series of qualitative interviews held between the author and a sample of psychoanalysts, this book examines both the unconscious experience and the interpersonal field of survivor siblings. Through a trauma-informed contemporary psychoanalytic lens, Dobrich combines data analysis, theory-building, memoir, and clinical storytelling to explore and explicate the impact of lateral survivorship on the clinical moment, making room for a contemporary and nuanced appreciation of siblings in psychoanalysis.

Working with Survivor Siblings in Psychoanalysis: Ability and Disability in Clinical Process will be of immense interest and value to psychoanalysts and other mental health professionals, and for all therapists who work with and treat patients who are themselves survivor siblings. Uniquely integrating both academic and memoir writing, this book will also engage those building theories around the implications of the analyst's subjectivity on clinical processes.

Johanna Dobrich is a licensed clinical social worker and psychoanalyst in private practice in New York City specializing in the treatment of dissociative disorders, trauma, and loss/bereavement. She teaches postgraduate courses and supervises those in advanced training at the Psychoanalytic Psychotherapy Study Center (PPSC), the Institute for Contemporary Psychotherapy (ICP), and the National Institute for the Psychotherapies in New York City.

Relational perspectives book series
Lewis Aron, Adrienne Harris,
Series Editors
Steven Kuchuck & Eyal Rozmarin

The Relational Perspectives Book Series (RPBS) publishes books that grow out of or contribute to the relational tradition in contemporary psychoanalysis. The term *relational psychoanalysis* was first used by Greenberg and Mitchell[1] to bridge the traditions of interpersonal relations, as developed within interpersonal psychoanalysis and object relations, as developed within contemporary British theory. But, under the seminal work of the late Stephen A. Mitchell, the term "*relational psychoanalysis*" grew and began to accrue to itself many other influences and developments. Various tributaries – interpersonal psychoanalysis, object relations theory, self-psychology, empirical infancy research, and elements of contemporary Freudian and Kleinian thought – flow into this tradition, which understands relational configurations between self and others, both real and fantasied, as the primary subject of psychoanalytic investigation.

We refer to the relational tradition, rather than to a relational school, to highlight that we are identifying a trend, a tendency within contemporary psychoanalysis, not a more formally organized or coherent school or system of beliefs. Our use of the term *relational* signifies a dimension of theory and practice that has become salient across the wide spectrum of contemporary psychoanalysis. Now under the editorial supervision of Adrienne Harris, Steven Kuchuck, and Eyal Rozmarin, the Relational Perspectives Book Series originated in 1990 under the editorial eye of the late Stephen A. Mitchell. Mitchell was the most prolific and influential of the originators of the relational tradition. Committed to dialogue among psychoanalysts, he abhorred the authoritarianism that dictated adherence to a rigid set of beliefs or technical restrictions. He championed open discussion and comparative and integrative approaches, and promoted new voices across the generations.

Included in the Relational Perspectives Book Series are authors and works that come from within the relational tradition, extend and develop that tradition, as well as works that critique relational approaches or compare and contrast it with alternative points of view. The series includes our most distinguished senior psychoanalysts, along with younger contributors who bring fresh vision. A full list of titles in this series is available at www.routledge.com/mentalhealth/series/LEARPBS.

1 Greenberg, J., & Mitchell, S. (1983). *Object relations in psychoanalytic theory*. Harvard University Press.

Working with Survivor Siblings in Psychoanalysis

Ability and Disability in Clinical Process

Johanna Dobrich

Routledge
Taylor & Francis Group

LONDON AND NEW YORK

First published 2021
by Routledge
2 Park Square, Milton Park, Abingdon, Oxon OX14 4RN

and by Routledge
52 Vanderbilt Avenue, New York, NY 10017

Routledge is an imprint of the Taylor & Francis Group, an informa business

© 2021 Johanna Dobrich

The right of Johanna Dobrich to be identified as author of this work has been asserted by her in accordance with sections 77 and 78 of the Copyright, Designs and Patents Act 1988.

British Library Cataloguing-in-Publication Data
A catalogue record for this book is available from the British Library

Library of Congress Cataloging-in-Publication Data
A catalog record for this book has been requested

ISBN: 978-0-367-64575-5 (hbk)
ISBN: 978-0-367-64576-2 (pbk)
ISBN: 978-1-003-12526-6 (ebk)

Typeset in Times New Roman
by Apex CoVantage, LLC

For Leo, so that you find the words for it.

Contents

Prologue

Survivor sibling reveries

The room is mostly dark with drifts of light coming through the translucent panels on the bedroom shade meant to minimize its impact. The mattress below me, finally firm enough to hold my weight and the hallucinatory infant that still resides in a sleep-induced fragment of my mind, laying between my partner and me who, before the recent purchase of this mattress, was at constant risk of accidental suffocation – swallowing of baby by cushion. Our actual son is asleep in his crib in the room next door. I drift off to sleep. I seem to take for granted now that I can drift off to sleep without much trouble.

Sometimes it is just an hour later, other times it is more than four. Or most cumbersome of all, perhaps it is only twenty minutes after my falling asleep that my young son's cries pierce my dreaming self and I am awake. The hallucinatory infant's cries used to wake me up too, but thankfully approaching my son's second birthday it is just my son's *actual* cries that pull me to consciousness. I feel my body tense up to meet a string of words more prayer than poem, heard inside my head as "*no no no – make it stop.*" As if I can will intrusion away by maintaining a strong front. I immediately recognize the prayer as familiar, echoing in my mindscape from the very beginnings of my consciousness. I glance at the alarm clock and quickly calculate how much time has passed from my being asleep to awake. As I'm doing the math, the "*no no no*" recedes into maternal recognition: *I am mom, not baby, mom will respond to a crying baby, mom MUST respond to a crying baby.* (I cannot allow for a world in which mom doesn't respond.) Mom checks the clock now to track the time and to make sure the intervention of going in and providing reassurance will not disrupt all the good growth baby's managed with self-soothing back to sleep. I say to myself, if he cries more than five minutes, I will go to him.

And then I assess the pattern of sounds and sighs he makes during those five minutes. Is it a continuous wail? If so, I am sitting up in bed, one foot already dangling off the side of the too-firm but yet safe mattress prepared to overthrow this rationale regime of fostering self-soothing skills and run into the room to pick up, hold, and contain his anguish (and my own). If it's on-and-off-again crying at a low pitch and interspersed with some other sounds, I hear it as speech. Maybe he's relaying his dream to himself? Maybe he wants an audience of mom to share it with? I don't need to sit up, as historically I know this usually trails off, leading him back to the path of sleep. But I begin to feel my own anxiety and wish for him to refind sleep soon, so that I can do the same. If the crying dissipates and it grows quiet again, my feet will not have touched the floor below, but my mind will be on like the lights in a theatre house, illuminating everything on the stage below. And as he presumably finds sleep, and as my partner resumes sleep with enviable ease, my thoughts will drift to my girlhood bed and back to the voice in my head saying *no no no*.

I feel particularly tortured by this sequence of what is just an ordinary experience of parenting babies. It is not his need for me itself (whether it is real, imagined, or projected in these moments) that is truly troubling. But awakening to the sound of my son's cries sets off an automatic bodily memory of hearing my severely disabled brother's cries overnight in girlhood. The uncertainty of *when it will happen, if it will happen, how many times it will happen, and how bad it will be for us both*, all evoke the terror of my own first six years of life, in which my older quadriplegic brother with spastic cerebral palsy would frequently have severe life-threatening seizures over the course of the night. This primitive part of me screams out in my head, *make it stop* in the present tense, even if other parts of me know that now is not then. This part cannot distinguish then from now, no matter how much time passes. The time of day most people come to associate with safety and restoration, even though separation plays a part in bedtime, was for me instead infused with unpredictable dread. The sounds coming from my brother's room, the sight of his clenched, shaking body, flesh turning purple and red, blood dripping down from lips caught by his teeth in the terror of the moment, his eyes wide open and dilated, and the attendant uncertainty about whether it would end with or without medical intervention, whether we'd be speeding in a screaming ambulance to the ER or expected to drift back to sleep. Scanning my mother's face for the truth of what might come next, and finding a drill sergeant barking commands "Joey go get me some water, help me move him here" and later,

"Go get me the Depakene," in her place. Or worse, sometimes she'd be drained of all feeling and eerily calm in the face of possible death. No drill sergeant, no worry, just the presence of a buzzing pitch, like the sounds the cicadas made in the Jersey summer nights.

In the morning, breakfast was made and had. Dogs were walked, and parents were dressed for work and sipping coffee, as I prepared for whatever the day had in store for me. We did not discuss the night terror episodes unless my brother had been admitted to the hospital, in which case it was referenced as something requiring coverage: "I'll go to the hospital from here and then to the office." Maybe that's not exactly true, maybe my mom checked in with me, but I never felt it as *a real* invitation to elaborate on my agony, fear, and anguish, my complete sensory overload of these scenes, my too-young growing recognition that sustaining life was not something any of us could take for granted, ever.

I do not know how many times this event happened. More than three times, but not once a week or anything like that. My son wakes and cries overnight far more often, I am sure, than my brother had life-threatening seizures when I was a child. But the frequency and unconscious association have very little to do with one another. And so it goes, that after my son in present time falls back asleep, I lay awake remembering the feel of my childhood carpet – a thick, soft, lush purple rug beneath my feet – as I leapt from my room to my brother's; the feel of the smooth, glossy wooden surface of the bedpost in my parent's room, where I'd hold on as I watched my mom tend to my brother in his beleaguered and frightening state, ready to meet her coming demands. I'll catch glimpses of the too-dark backyard, which could be seen from the kitchen window where I'd be fetching the water from the sink for my brother. I'll feel the pull of outside, how the darkness in those moments both offered me an escape and a terror that it could swallow me whole, that I could disappear into it and no one would know I was gone because the crisis with my brother was occupying everyone's attention.

Flashing forward as a psychoanalyst now, I listen to patients and note both the present and absent ways in which siblings are considered primary characters in their life narratives. I believe my calling to listen in this very particular way meets my own unending need to even the score between my speechless brother and myself. To make a bridge between the verbal land in which I have always lived and the one he never has. This book seeks to take that journey a step further in compiling a narrative study of the stories of psychoanalysts who, like me, grew up alongside a severely disabled sibling.

The aim of this book is to examine a particular kind of relational sphere and experience that has not received enough of our collective attention. What happens to a person's sense of self, both personally and professionally, when they grow up alongside a severely disabled sibling? What does it mean for a survivor sibling, whose early life is filled with sensory, cognitive and affective awareness regarding their disabled sibling's capacities, as well as their shared caregiver's narcissistic injuries, to dedicate themselves to a vocation that hopes for human growth? What can be understood about the relationship between survival of this kind and the practice of psychoanalysis? Relational psychoanalysis takes seriously the developmental achievement of subjectivity and centers recognition at the heart of optimal human relatedness. Achieving a separate sense of self, alongside an understanding of the subjectivity of others in the family, while outpacing one's disabled sibling, has enormous intrapsychic and interpersonal consequences that can be felt across the lifetime of the survivor sibling. Survivor siblings are often left in the position of representing their own internal psychic reality and the unmentalized reality of their disabled sibling. They can come to feel haunted by the unlived but witnessed experience of their sibling in ways that shape them well beyond the early experience itself.

In general, sibling relationships have not been given the same degree of theoretical or clinical consideration within the psychoanalytic literature as the parental or caregiving systems in which children are raised. But more specifically, the presumption within the limited sibling literature that lateral relationship goals center on negotiating space between and within the self, oftentimes implies a belief of equal capacity which leaves out of its theorizing cases of sibling pairings where unmatched potentials due to medical conditions are present right from the very start. A twin-ship of health and its shocking and total absence skews the normative questions typically asked regarding rivalry for excellence and winning parent's attention into another territory. This book speaks to this absence with presence.

This book examines the themes and developmental experiences relayed to me through the process of interviewing 15 psychoanalysts who meet the criteria of survivor sibling. A survivor sibling is someone for whom the medical history of the compromised sibling was chronic and had a serious effect on psychological, physical, and social development (e.g., Down syndrome, genetic disorders, and cerebral palsy). The criteria for inclusion are the presence of a sibling whose medical issue was incurable and present from early on in the developmental life cycle, with persisting disabling features. The sample was obtained on a volunteer basis following a query from me sent to the following psychoanalytic community listservs: The International Association for Relational Psychoanalysis and Psychotherapy (IARPP), Division 39, and the American Association for Psychoanalysis in Clinical Social Work (AAPCSW). The sample included 14 female analysts and one male analyst of varying ages and demographic backgrounds.[1] I do not know what variable/s to attribute to the over-representation of female analysts in the sample. Perhaps cultural sanctioning and socialization toward sharing vulnerability and the practice of it over one's lifetime make female respondents *more likely* to participate in such a study as compared to their male counterparts? Another possibility is that a greater percentage of survivor sibling psychoanalysts are female, but I do not have the empirical data or means to confirm this hypothesis. Given the over-representation of female respondents, the findings are skewed toward a sister's experience of survivorship, though it is impossible to say how important the gendered dimension of this experience is without being able to compare it to something else.

Each participant engaged in a semi-structured qualitative interview with the author that focused on two thematic pathways: subjective developmental outcomes in survivorship and their impact on the clinical moment. Regarding the clinical moment, experiences both as a patient and as an analyst were examined. While each participant was ultimately asked the same series of questions, the timing, cadence and flow of association varied with each interview. Because it is a narrative study and because as an author, I consider my own subjective experience as relevant, the format of this book will be an unusual compilation of storytelling, clinical exposition and theory building. I share a lot more of my own personal narrative than is usually included in our clinical literature, though recent trends have moved in this direction (Farber, 2017; Kuchuck, 2014; Gerson, 1996).

I'm not the first – and I am certain I will not be the last – analyst to raise the question why siblings are so little considered in our theories of both human development and mental disease/stress (Agger, 1988; Safer, 2002; Mitchell, 2003; Coles, 2003; Silverman, 2006; Vivona, 2007; Cornell, 2013; Grand, 2018). In a sense, the field is wide open for contributions to be made. In this book, I seek to answer a piece of the puzzle in exploring firsthand data from practicing psychoanalysts about the relationship between their work and their histories of being survivor siblings. This promises not only to broaden self-understanding for those who carry a legacy of survivorship but also to help analysts of all stripes actively mentalize the complexities and nuances within the sibling experience as an ongoing part of our clinical work. It is also my hope to speak to the void in which this kind of experience with survivorship often resides, through an analysis of personal narratives.

References

Agger, E. M. (1988). Psychoanalytic perspectives on sibling relationships. *Psychoanalytic Inquiry*, 83–30.

Coles, P. (2003). *The importance of sibling relationships in psychoanalysis*. Karnac Books Ltd.

Cornell, W. (2013). Lost and found: Sibling loss, disconnection, mourning and intimacy. In A. Frank, P. T. Clough, & S. Siedman (Eds.), *Intimacies: A new world of relational life* (pp. 130–145). Routledge.

Farber, S. K. (Ed.). (2017). *Celebrating the wounded healer psychotherapist: Pain, post-traumatic growth and self-disclosure*. Routledge.

Gerson, B. (Ed.). (1996). *The therapist as a person: Life crises, life choices, life experience and their effects on treatment*. The Analytic Press.

Grand, S. (2018). Trauma as radical inquiry. In L. Aron, S. Grand, & J. Slochower (Eds.), *Decentering relational theory* (pp. 5–27). Routledge.

Kuchuck, S. (Ed.). (2014). *Clinical implications of the psychoanalyst's life experience: When the personal becomes professional*. Routledge.

Mitchell, J. (2003). *Siblings*. Polity Press.

Safer, J. (2002). *The normal one: Life with a difficult or damaged sibling*. The Free Press.

Silverman, S. (2006). Where we both have lived. *Psychoanalytic Dialogues, 165*, 527–542.

Vivona, J. (2007). Sibling differentiation, identity development and the lateral dimension of psychic life. *Journal of the American Psychoanalytic Association, 55*(4), 1191–1215.

Note

1 A few additional male subjects did respond to the initial query, but either did not meet the full criteria for inclusion in the study *or* in another case presented with an extensive survivorship history that included so many other variables beyond the sibling dimension that a focus on siblingship, in particular, was not possible. As far as other demographic details go, specific details are omitted to preserve the privacy of the participants – but participants range in age (from 32 to 80), socio-economic status, region of residence/country of origin, level of training/experience and religious/cultural/racial background.

Acknowledgments

This book could not have come together without the support of family, friends and colleagues. Lindsay – thanks for believing in this project from the very beginning and reminding me when I'd "forgotten" how important it was to see it through. Thanks to Steven Kuchuck for helping me find and craft my own psychoanalytic voice. I'm indebted to Hannah Wright and Rebecca Pringle at Routledge and Andrea Fortunato Loftus for the provision of their instructive editorial contributions. A heartfelt thanks to Leslie, whose attuned presence altered my interior in profound ways. To Eli Zal, Yamille Mason, Patricia Clough, Holly Levenkron, and Susan Gair for all the emotional and intellectual support along the way. To my partner and child, for tolerating my absence while I got lost and found, and lost again – in the writing. To my parents, for providing everything they had to give. To Teddy and Oliver for sharing in the experience of siblingship with me. To all those committed to repairing the wounds of development. And finally, to the survivor siblings themselves for being brave enough to participate in this project making their vulnerability a source of learning for us all.

Chapter 1

Psychoanalytic reflections of sibling experience

Introduction

Little has been written about the place of siblings in the psychoanalytic family, either clinically or conceptually, and even less from a Relational perspective (Grand, 2018). The representation of the sibling register within the transference and countertransference experience, and in our psychic structures at different levels of analysis more broadly, often remains unelaborated. Factoring in the presence of severe disability and difference among siblings narrows the existing pool of literature within the psychoanalytic canon further (Safer, 2002). As psychoanalysts, we are less theoretically primed to think along a lateral relational dimension, barring some notable exceptions (Agger, 1988; Coles, 2003; Balsam, 2013; Bodansky, 2014; Grand, 2018; Kieffer, 2008; Mitchell, 2003, 2013; Orange, 2014; Rosner, 1985; Ruiz, 2012; Safer, 2002; Silverman, 2006; Sullivan, 1954; Vivona, 2010). Attending to events along the lateral relational dimension of developmental life and noticing the implications on psychic functioning, sense of self, and relatedness to others is entering unchartered waters. It can feel as if the ghost of Freud hangs heavy when we start to dream up and imagine relational dimensions of life that may be felt to displace or compete with the centrality of the Oedipal story. But a look into lateral relations need not imply an evasion of our more familiar vertical axis, as these registers interact and infiltrate one another within relational life and unconscious experience (Mitchell, 2003, 2013).

When I turned to the literature to better understand psychoanalytic perspectives on the place of siblings in our inner and outer lives, the epistemological orientation from which the papers were written did not resonate with the experience of being a survivor sibling. In this chapter, I will summarize the theoretical perspectives I encountered in the search and then go on to introduce the clinical concepts I find most resonant in making sense of sibling survivorship. Influenced by the trauma literature on dissociative disorders, the neuroscience of attachment, and the exploratory clinical acumen of a contemporary relational psychoanalytic practice, I consider how the dissociation and assimilation of ambiguous loss affect the survivor sibling within the family system and later in their vocational practice (Boss, 1999; Bromberg, 1998; Siegel, 1999; Van Der Hart et al., 2006). The impact of survivorship results in a plethora of what I call *unexperienced-experience* with developmental sequelae that call for a revisionary and nuanced understanding of the clinical process. I hope to generate psychoanalytic thinking about the importance of attending to trauma along the lateral relational dimension, as well as enhance clinicians' capacities for mutual recognition of a register that often remains unformulated within our field (Stern, 1983).

Relational perspectives on theory building

The Relational turn in psychoanalysis altered the epistemological context in which psychoanalytic theory is made. We are no longer inclined to create grand theory and generalize developmental or clinical findings into linear, stage-driven, positivistic structures with discrete categorizations of health and its absence. Health and subjectivity exist more along a continuum of loosely constrained but affiliated dialectical tensions (Mitchell, 1988; Mitchell & Aron, 1999; Ogden, 1989). A relational sensibility does not valorize unconscious content, as if it can only be gleamed from dreams or our patient's "free" associations (Mitchell, 1988). Freed up from interpreting everything through a drive-derivative lens, we no longer split primitive from non-primitive defenses along pejorative lines regarding "analyzability." Nor do we pre-suppose a unitary subject, as the notion of a singular (sense of) self is replaced with a non-unitary structure that contains a multiplicity of self/other configurations which, taken together, come to feel like "me" (Bromberg, 1993).

One way I identify a Relational sensibility is one that bypasses dichotomous thinking, welcoming instead contradiction and paradox (Pizer, 1992). Transcending polarities invites a deep dive into the unique encounter as it occurs both within (object relations) and between people (interpersonal relations) and their psyches/somas (Aron, 1991; Mitchell, 1988; Ogden, 1994). The experience itself contains all polarities and dualities simultaneously ("good"/"bad"/"neutral," conscious/uncon-scious, doer/done to, fantasized/experienced, etc.) whether or not a person has the capacity to attend to every dimension (Benjamin, 2004). We now thankfully take for granted that the observed is necessarily impacted by the observer and vice versa in a continuous bidirectional fashion (Hoffman, 1991).

This does not leave us without any options for theorizing, though centering human subjectivity and its vicissitudes in relation to various dyads/triads/societal/cultural domains and levels of consciousness make it impossible to say something that is generalizable to all. Instead, our attention shifts to how environments (intra- and inter-) create and curtail potentialities for growth and change within and between people. Relational approaches incidentally generate theory specifying these optimal intra- and inter-relational conditions on the basis of the lived experience between people, most importantly including how the interpersonal field allows for and constrains such change and movement. It lets go of the illusion that "the well" are categorically different from "the sick," and distills developmental experience as something that is accessible within the clinical moment *between* two people, as opposed to an archeological dig into the past through the one-way street of a patient's verbally represented unconscious (Levenson, 2009). It makes use of all dimensions of time – past, present, and future – and ignites and enlists imagination as a powerful source of healing. In the words of Emmanuel Ghent (1992), "Relational theorists tend to share a view in which both reality and fantasy, both outer world and inner world, both the interpersonal and the intrapsychic, play immensely important and interactive roles in human life" (p. xvii). In short, it unsettles what was once considered psychoanalysis (Mitchell, 1988). I share this paradigm shift to orient the reader to my experience. When I set out to examine the existing literature on siblings and siblingship within the psychoanalytic canon, I mostly encountered data obtained from a pre-Relational one-person perspective, where the author(s) offered broadly assumed generalizable observations about the unconscious role of siblings in a patient's psychic life, absent an appreciation for the bidirectional field in which these observations were cast. The information gathered from this vantage point felt quite limiting in studying survivor siblings, most of all because they are not represented. These earlier papers assume evenness in capacities among children and focus on the intrapsychic consequences of jealousy, rivalry, and aggression as they are expressed in the inner object world through the transference. A more nuanced understanding of what a survivor sibling may feel vis-à-vis their disabled sibling, including these internalized object representations as well as the "real" relationship, is eclipsed. Despite these limitations, I think it's important to cover the tracks that were laid before I offer other ways of engaging the sibling dimension. But I want to caution the reader that to look at the impact of severely disabled siblings on survivor siblings does not necessitate and actually cannot result in a new grand theory or complex. A Relational perspective is not a theory but a sensibility (Mitchell & Aron, 1999). And it sensitizes us to context and the complex, unpredictable, but always ongoing relationship between permeable boundaried levels of unconscious and conscious experience within and between selves. My goal is not to set forth a diagnostic category of survivor siblings but to apply careful attention to the experience of survivorship in this lateral context, as it is relayed to me. I hope to leave readers with a strong affective impression and many more questions, rather than a diagnostic category itself. But first, let's see what some elder analytic author siblings had to say on the matter.

History speaks through relationship

In researching this book, I came across the autobiographical fact that both Freud and Ferenczi experienced the death of younger siblings during their early years (Berman, 2004). Perhaps that's not so unusual given the rate of infant mortality for their time. But given how foundational their impassioned and strenuous relationship to one another has been to our discipline, I found it really interesting to consider how their differing reactions to this shared autobiographical experience contributed to their theoretical stances. Whereas Freud focused on the competitive strivings between siblings for parental attention, Berman makes the case that Ferenczi went in the direction of a co-conspirator and collaborator. Berman's close reading of the correspondence between Freud and Ferenczi delineates the latter's openness to inhabiting lateral relations within the transference and countertransference field, alongside the more familiar hierarchal relations. Freud, it seemed, was aligned with authority; Ferenczi, with his peers. Berman (2004) suggests that in Ferenczi's exploration of "mutual analysis":

> Ferenczi shifted his central therapeutic image from mothers and children to brothers and sisters. Parents are out of the picture, Analyst and

analysand are now Hansel and Gretel, seeking hand in hand their lost path in a dark forest populated by abusive witches.

(p. 50)

Contemporary (re)discoveries of Ferenczi's thinking and clinical practice reveal his creativity in using his own vulnerability as a guide (Dupont, 1988; Ferenczi, 1988). A less hierarchical and more lateral relatedness were experimented with on the basis of felt clinical necessity. Importantly, this was tied to his capacity to appreciate how trauma shaped and warped human identity, making him sensitive to the registers of power between patient and analyst/child/parent, all the while living this traumatic love relationship out with Freud (Ferenczi, 1949). It seems that Ferenczi opened the door to a psychoanalytic appreciation of lateral relations. It is beyond the scope of this book to offer a full summary of this psychoanalytic history, but I want to note that Ferenczi's contributions included a path toward lateral relatedness that was dislocated in time as the relationship between him and Freud ultimately orphaned Ferenczi's clinical legacy from the generations of analysts that came after him (Harris & Kuchuck, 2014). Perhaps Freud's commitment from 1900 onward to the Oedipus complex as the defining feature of family life constrained our psychoanalytic imaginations, even as it broke new ground in demonstrating the power of unconscious phenomena in the parent/child relationship.

"One Person" instinctually driven views on siblings

The resulting hegemonic loyalty to Freud necessitated analytic attention on Oedipal strivings and object relations built up around these vertical power relations. An instinctual view of unconscious life is guided by the belief that internal objects interface with drive derivatives through fantasy, creating character structure, and shaping the course development. Siblings become powerful objects of rivalry and contrast, yielding an unconscious effect on identity formation through competition and comparison. Lateral relations offer the unconscious a playground in which to try on various identifications/counter-identifications under less psychic threat than may be felt with parents (Charles, 1999; Rosner, 1985). Charles (1999) asserts that taking these risks is less threatening internally than engaging in these struggles with authority figures.

Juliet Mitchell (2003, 2013), the premiere psychoanalytic sibling theorist who disrupts the centrality placed on the Oedipal drama, puts forth a universal theory of sibling's unconscious psychic trauma of displacement. The feared displacement a new baby ignites in a sibling is thought to accompany intense feelings of love and hatred that can easily overwhelm a not matured ego. Mitchell highlights the mutative affect of the mother's role in "seriality," sending the unconscious communication of there being room for more than one child in her heart. Absent seriality, these traumatic unconscious affects remain potent. Vivona (2010) applies this larger theoretical formulation to her clinical work with a patient who utilizes the transference to move back and forth through sibling-to-sibling and parent-to-child relations in establishing a unique identity of her own. Vivona describes inherent difficulties as the patient works to transform feelings of hatred and eroticism toward a sibling into a matured identity of her own (Vivona, 2010). With a Kleinian flavor, the task of integrating opposing feelings toward the object is thought to enhance one's own identity/psychic maturity. Vivona does not explicitly use her countertransference in the work, but she does draw our attention to the sibling dimension as the patient encounters it. Balsam (2013) also offers an in-depth clinical account and describes how difficulties in creativity tied to static sibling relationships with an undifferentiated mother can wreak psychic havoc.

In an effort to legitimize the place and consideration of siblings in our unconscious life within psychoanalysis, Legorreta, Levaque, and Levinsky-Wohl (2013) argue that there is something called a "sibling complex" with universal implications. This dimension of psychic life is represented by "the internalization of feelings, attitudes and behaviors related to sibling-as-objects" (p. 173), independent of actual siblings, and shows up in twinning transferences, instinctual life, defenses, and character structure. They also highlight that it can be seen at the cultural level in the cohort experience – where they credit Freud, for their initial formulation that sibling rivalries may be tempered on the basis of a joint resistance to the father, which they argue is the underlying foundation of all fraternal systems (p. 173).

My experience in reading these papers left me feeling confused and unsure about writing this book. Feelings of competition and envy are the last place my psyche goes when I think of my severely disabled brother and his impact on my subjectivity. It's not that they are entirely absent, but certainly not *most* resonant and when present, are not in the form we ordinarily expect them to take shape among siblings. What did it mean that I was unable to integrate these perspectives or find an affective home in them? It felt like reading in a different language. Was it simply a difference in theoretical allegiance blocking my capacity to make use of these ideas, or something more? I later came to see that it is a privilege to compete with a sibling. The severity and reality of disability and illness make unconscious themes of competition and eroticism less relevant than they might otherwise be. The themes presented seemed utterly devoid of any familiar affective landscape and left me feeling alien, and in conducting the interviews I realized I was not alone.

As I read more contemporary expressions of sibling experience, I encountered Bodansky's (2014) paper, which locates siblings experientially somewhere between inner and outer reality, and describes the protective aspect of siblings' influence on one another in developing caregiving motivational systems. Siblings who can mirror and regulate one another's emotional experience help prevent psychic breakdown when the parents are unable to do so. However, while these perspectives felt more theoretically relevant, the capacity to co-regulate between siblings of such disparate capacities still did not speak to the survivor sibling landscape or the larger familial context in which it is held. Nevertheless, Bodansky is the first to demonstrate clinically how siblings may mentalize one another's experience, thereby serving a containing function in one another's lives. We can extend this notion of co-regulation and mentalization into the therapeutic dyad.

Contemporary laterality

If historically siblings were not focused on in psychoanalysis because of political fears in decentering the influence of the Oedipal complex, I think contemporarily our blind spots have more to do with the impact of unformulated experience than anything else (Kieffer, 2008; Stern, 1983). We cannot represent that which has not taken shape. A few others have treaded where I aim to go in a relational sense, though not specifically zoning in on survival siblings per say. A highly simplified notion of Sullivan's (1954) development of interpersonal psychoanalysis illuminates the analyst's role in recognizing a patient's "obscure difficulties in living" and how these self/other-deceptions "interpenetrate all aspects of [a patient's] current interpersonal relationships" thereby making room for, and use of, lateral relationships as formative events (pp. 14–15). Traumatic sibling relationships can cross generations the same way that dysfunctional attachment patterns can, and taking a transgenerational view of sibling relationships is highly relevant to relational practice (Coles, 2007; Grand & Salberg, 2017). Kieffer (2008) reviews the unique contributions of serial relations beyond the often-noted aspect of rivalry and identity, to include the mirroring and regulatory features of these connections holding both sides of a relational potential in the same frame (p. 161). She goes on to show how siblingship in the analytic encounter is cocreated by analyst and patient together. Orange (2014), in response to Bodansky's claim that siblings can transmute the developmental arrest of one another through mentalization, offers a relational view of siblings as both prospective trauma transmitters and protectors and that a parallel potentiality exists within the sibling transference/countertransference medium (p. 251).

Grand (2018), an expert at weaving the intrapsychic with the collective registers, considers how mentalization, resilience, and enduring love have not had the same focus as destruction, failed witnessing, and caregivers' lack in the context of studying trauma relationally. She points out *"the missing siblings are particularly problematic for constructing a field theory of traumatic resiliency"* and by "siblings," includes all peer relations, inside and adjacent to one's family (p. 15). By asking what exists *beyond* the maternal dyad and Oedipal triangles, Grand is calling our attention to the cohort dimension in order to better understand resiliency.

Survivor sibling perspectives

Implied in most of the literature is an assumed evenness among capacities within the sibling experience or later onset of mental deterioration or sudden death of an otherwise healthy sibling (Bodansky, 2014; Cornell, 2013; Silverman, 2006). While there may be differences in dispositions or innate talents among siblings, all of which have ramifications for their relationship to each other and to parental attention, most of the literature is not assuming a sibling encounters a devastatingly medically complex compatriot in their world. Siblings who lose an otherwise healthy sibling to premature death have been studied, and research reveals that a caregiver's coherence around the loss is a predictive determinant of the surviving siblings psychic well-being (Fanos, 1996; O'Leary & Gaziano, 2011; Pollock, 1986).

Two notable exceptions that look specifically at the psychosocial well-being of survivor siblings who grow up around and with knowledge of their medically complex sibling/s are not specifically psychoanalytic papers.

However, in the aggregate data, they offer a compelling thematic profile of survivorship, which includes being at greater risk than control groups for: Illnesses that affect daily functioning and internalizing symptoms, survival guilt, defective fears, weaknesses associated with help-seeking, guilt and shame around negative feelings toward peers, compulsive altruism, and guardedness about family difficulties (Barlow & Ellard, 2006; Caplan, 2011). Caplan (2011) studied and treated college-aged survivor siblings who sought counseling while at university and drew similar conclusions around survivor sibling's difficulties, acknowledging ambivalence toward family members, revising systems of compulsory caretaking, and enacting the impact of emotional neglect in the transference by being the "good" patient.

Perhaps the most well-known psychoanalytic perspective on the topic to date comes from Jeanne Safer (2002), who wrote "The Normal One: Life with a Difficult or Damaged Sibling," in which she developed a universal profile of "intact siblings" unconscious experience and self-identity based on interviews of "normal ones." In her sample, Safer does not distinguish between siblings of those with difficult personalities from siblings of those with severe physical or intellectual disability. Safer describes "Caliban Syndrome" as a set of personality traits characteristic of the "normal" siblings, which include premature maturity, compulsion to achieve, survivor guilt, and fear of contagion.

Identifying the theoretical landscape: putting survivor siblings in context

Dissociative structure and ambiguous loss

What is the experience of *being* a sibling in relation to a severely disabled sibling like?

I hope to flesh out the context illuminating how this lateral relation gets experienced (or not experienced, as it were) both interpersonally and intrapsychically within a survivor sibling from a phenomenological and contextual perspective (Stolorow & Atwood, 2002). I adopt a trauma-informed developmental lens in seeking to examine the legacy of survivorship among siblings. I am aware that in choosing this framework I am necessarily highlighting certain aspects of the experience and minimizing others.[1]

Rather than find the unthought known (Bollas, 1987), I am looking to illuminate the contextual impact of what I call *unexperienced-experience* (Dobrich, 2020). As is well established in the trauma literature, dissociation and survival are tightly linked – and because the presence of a chronic, often life-threatening and always life-limiting, condition in a family member creates a traumatic loss to everyone involved, we'd expect dissociation to play a large role in a family's capacity to adapt. A consequence of surviving this way is the absence of an elaborated presence; an ongoing, mediated sense of the experience *having happened* along with the attendant paradoxical interior experience of it still "happening" inside a survivor. When I say "unexperienced-experience," I am referring to disruptions in the registration of consciously encountered sensorial events themselves, as well as the attendant unconscious fears, wishes, and fantasies – the inner elaborations that accompany them. The memories of experiences need not be totally absent to meet the criteria of unexperienced-experience, as I view the capacity to really inhabit our experience along a continuum as opposed to a discrete variable. This continuum ranges from a highly inhabitable one – where the experience is felt as *having happened to me*, and it's past meaning, present impact, and future narrative are all felt as accessible and impacting one's subjectivity – to the middle zone where the experience is unlinked and its cognitive, affective, and somatic contents are split apart, partially available for assimilation in the present tense, all the way to total dissociative amnesia where the experience seems not to have happened to any of one's selves at all. A survivor's spatial location on this barometer of the capacity to bear and inhabit experience can vary and is not static. I locate unexperienced-experience anywhere from someplace mid-range on the continuum up to the end of total absence/annihilation. This concept borrows heavily from both Winnicott's (1974) notion of a "fear of breakdown," D. B Stern's (1983) notion of unformulated experience and is made possible by Bromberg's (1998) vision regarding the multiplicity of self. This phenomenon is also well described in clinical practice by Bion, who notices how patients come to absent themselves from the acuity of their sensory experience and hatred of reality/ies through the use of dissociation (Bion, 2013).

Unexperienced-experience does not mean that none of the experience is encountered, but rather it's taken in, in pieces which may include sensory impressions, cognitive elaborations, and stories, affectively charged feelings, fantasy elements, as well as the observable data itself absent feeling. The complete experience is evaded by the splitting of the content into separate parts that together form a whole expanded rendering and encountering. Another attendant artifact of unexperienced-experience is the discontinuity in self-states it may generate as a by-product of the splitting of the experience itself. Self-states house the internal working models of specific relationships, so splitting apart these identifications, rendering some more conscious than others, may be one way to manage an experience that crosses the threshold of bearability. It is of course a fantasy, the idea of wholeness, or the notion of reaching total integration and presence of self with any experience in its totality, but unexperienced-experience is different from the experience that is inhabited because the fragmentation disrupts mentalization forging and solidifying a reliance on a dissociative structure. Striving to both inhabit and potentially integrate unexperienced-experiences is often the foundational bedrock upon which psychic healing can occur. This book explores what conditions facilitate such encounters among survivor siblings.

Survivors break the unbearable into barely manageable bits and are left with a plethora of unexperienced-experience as they grow into adults. If you accept this initial condition as a preliminary likelihood of what is asked of a survivor sibling in adapting to living out the legacy of being abled vis-à-vis their sibling, the sequela of what follows is as unique as a piece of artwork. I do not claim that any two survivors survived the same or put forth an essentialist or universalizing profile. Some other books have done so (Safer, 2002), and while there may be themes that resonate, we could never say that any two survivors share all the same qualities or capacities or that they universally adapted a singular character structure. As you'll hear from the narratives that unfold, having survived is the common thread, but then *how* is as variable as we are human.

Defining disability along experiential lines of the sibling's subjectivity

This book is for and about the interior lives of survivor siblings. It is not written for the caregivers or the disabled themselves. If it were, I might not have adopted a trauma-informed lens, and I would be unlikely to situate a framework of disability as a loss. If this were a book aimed at social justice or raising the consciousness of others regarding the humanity of the disabled, I would definitely have adopted a different framework. I admire the advocacy research that centers on humanizing difference and growing tolerance. I am well-versed experientially in the importance of building inclusive humanity for us all. I am inner-dialoging with Andrew Solomon (2012, 2019) on this issue right now as these words pour onto the page. But because it's for the survivor siblings themselves, whose inner experience is rarely, if at all, represented elsewhere, I hope you'll indulge me in adopting a traumatic loss framework to capture some of the experience of being abled in ways that one's sibling is not and will never be. I do not think this means the entirety of the experience is a loss. In fact, survivor siblings themselves give voice to what may be uniquely gained from loving a brother or sister who is severely disabled throughout this book. But there is already a lot of information out there that focuses on what the disabled have to teach the nondisabled about tolerance and differentness, and this book is for the survivor siblings who likely already have places to bring their feelings of pride and affiliation vis-à-vis their sibling relationship, but often lack any room to bring "negative" (self) states related to the experience, conscious or otherwise. The lack of reflectivity on their losses only further inculcates unexperienced-experience, reinforcing a reliance on dissociation – so I take it pretty seriously that focusing on what is lost is an important part of the theorizing here. But that does not mean that I define disability as loss, as much as I am trying to say that to be a survivor sibling is to negotiate a particular kind of loss as a part of one's identity.

What do I mean when I say loss? Family therapist Pauline Boss (1999) coined the term ambiguous loss, which she defines as situations in which: "people are perceived as physically absent but psychologically present because it's unclear whether they are alive or dead or when a person is perceived as physically present but psychologically absent" (pp. 8–9). The definition sounds simple enough but consider this passage:

> ambiguity complicates loss, it complicates the mourning process. People can't start grieving because the situation is indeterminate. It feels like a loss but it is not really one. The confusion freezes the grieving process. People plummet from hope to hopelessness and back again. Depression, anxiety, somatic illnesses often set in. The symptoms affect the individuals first, but can radiate in a ripple effect that impacts the whole family
>
> (pp. 10–11)

Ambiguity really captures the experience of not knowing what one is likely to encounter or deal with over time and how this experience invites a dissociative process. Because childhood disabilities of this severity unfold in real time, the full extent of what may be lost cannot be grasped in any one moment for anyone. As with any loss, we may not be able to fully feel what's at stake in a single moment, but there is a difference between things not fully felt and known, and things remaining unknown and not yet felt. In fact, many times, the severity of what's to come is masked by the presence of a seemingly typical infant with infant capacities. It is only with the passage of time that the differences in capacities and the seriousness of the medical conditions, which come to structure early family life, reveal themselves while the literal, physical, and psychic distance between siblings grows. Instead of growing up together, one outgrows or outpaces the other with no hope of arriving in adulthood together. Ambiguity pervades the experience as it becomes impossible in an ongoing way to know what to expect or to gain a definite picture of what goes on inside the disabled sibling's experience with any certainty. Boss (1999) conceptualizes a category for a kind of loss that cannot be met head-on because its form remains indeterminate and ongoing.

Conclusion

What is the effect of living alongside an ambiguous loss with one's peer like? How does this lateral world develop and unfold within survivor siblings and with what impact on the clinical moment? This book examines the intrapsychic and interpersonal legacy of such an experience, as well as the relationship between survivorship and the vocational practice of psychoanalysis. It builds on the growing Relational literature, which examines the connection between the lived experience of psychoanalysts and their clinical work and the impact of traumatic survival on an analytic stance (Farber, 2017; Gerson, 1996; Kuchuck, 2014). Come with me as I search for the voices and stories of fellow survivor siblings – all psychoanalytic psychotherapists who agreed to participate in this qualitative interview process with me. Listen as I catalogue my own experience alongside the voices of fifteen other clinicians who elected to be interviewed from all over the United States, as well as two subjects from Mexico and Brazil. Witness as we encountered together the unexperienced-experience in talking with one another (Chapter 2), and travel back in memory with us as we recollect/(re)construct what it was like when we first came to know of and appreciate some of the immediate impacts of this kind of loss in our lives (Chapter 3). Turn your attention toward the indelible effects on the attachment system between survivor siblings and their caregivers (Chapter 4). Listen to the siblings as they discern how they came to be psychoanalysts (Chapter 5) and what their experience of being a patient (Chapter 6) with this particular autobiographical experience was like, as well as how it impacts their work as clinicians (Chapter 7). Finally, think with me together as we consider the unknowable future and the long half-life of survivors of ambiguous loss on the generations to follow (Chapter 8).

Note

1 This awareness comes with trepidation about defining the experience of survivorship as traumatic being conflated with defining disability as trauma. The latter is not my intent, but by focusing on the former, I imagine it could be easily misconstrued.

References

Agger, E. M. (1988). Psychoanalytic perspectives on sibling relationships. *Psychoanalytic Inquiry*, *8*, 3–30.

Aron, L. (1991). The patient's experience of the analyst's subjectivity. *Psychoanalytic Dialogues*, *1*(1), 29–51.

Balsam, R. H. (2013). Sibling interaction. *Psychoanalytic Study of the Child*, *67*, 35–52.

Barlow, J., & Ellard, D. (2006). The psychosocial well-being of children with chronic disease, their parents and siblings: An overview of the research evidence base. *Child: Care, Health & Development*, *32*, 19–31.

Benjamin, J. (2004). Beyond doer and done to: An intersubjective view of thirdness. *Psychoanalytic Quarterly*, *73*(1), 5–46.

Berman, E. (2004). *Impossible training: A Relational view of psychoanalytic education*. The Analytic Press.

Bion, W. (2013). Second seminar – 14 April 1967. In J. Aguayo & B. Malin (Eds.), *Wilfred Bion: Los Angeles seminars and supervision*. Karnac.

Bodansky, R. (2014). Release from developmental arrest – Early childhood trauma: The case of Mrs. E. *Psychoanalytic Inquiry*, *34*(3), 191–203.

Bollas, C. (1987). *The shadow of the object: Psychoanalysis of the unthought known*. Columbia University Press.

Boss, P. (1999). *Ambiguous loss: Learning to live with unresolved grief*. Harvard University Press.

Bromberg, P. M. (1993). Shadow and substance: A relational perspective on clinical process. *Psychoanalytic Psychology*, *10*(2), 147–168.

Bromberg, P. M. (1998). *Standing in the spaces: Essays on clinical process, trauma & dissociation*. Analytic Press.

Caplan, R. (2011). Someone else can use this time more than me: Working with college students with impaired siblings. *Journal of College Student Psychotherapy*, *25*, 120–131.

Charles, M. (1999). Sibling mysteries: Enactments of unconscious fears & fantasies. *Psychoanalytic Review*, *86*(6), 877–901.

Coles, P. (2003). *The importance of sibling relationships in psychoanalysis*. Karnac Books Ltd.

Coles, P. (2007). Transgenerational conflicts between sisters. *British Journal of Psychotherapy*, *23*(4), 563–574. http://dx.doi.org.libproxy.newschool.edu/10.1111/j.1752-0118.2007.00051.x

Cornell, W. F. (2013). Lost and found: Sibling loss, disconnection, mourning and intimacy. In A. Frank, P. T. Clough, & S. Seidman (Eds.), *Intimacies: A new world of relational life* (pp. 130–145). Routledge.

Dobrich, J. (2020). An elegy for motherless daughters: Dissociation, multiplicity and mourning. *Psychoanalytic Perspectives, 17*(3), 366–384.

Dupont, J. (1988). Ferenczi's "madness." *Contemporary Psychoanalysis, 24*(2), 250–261. https://doi.org/10.1080/00107530.1988.10746240

Fanos, J. H. (1996). *Sibling loss*. Lawrence Erlbaum Associates Press.

Farber, S. (Ed.). (2017). *Celebrating the wounded healer psychotherapist: Pain, post-traumatic growth & self disclosure*. Routledge.

Ferenczi, S. (1949). Confusion of the tongues between the adults and the child: The language of tenderness and of passion. *International Journal of Psycho-Analysis, 30*, 225–230.

Ferenczi, S. (1988). *The clinical diary of Sandor Ferenczi*. Harvard University Press.

Gerson, B. (1996). *The therapist as a person: Life crises, life choices, life experiences and their effects on treatment*. The Analytic Press.

Ghent, E. (1992). Foreword. In N. J. Skolnick & S. C. Warshaw (Eds.), *Relational perspectives in psychoanalysis* (pp. xiii–xxii). The Analytic Press.

Grand, S. (2018). Trauma as Radical Inquiry. In L. Aron, S. Grand, & J. A. Slochower (Eds.), *Decentering relational theory: A comparative critique*. Routledge.

Grand, S., & Salberg, J. (2017). *Trans-generational trauma and the other: Dialogues across history & difference*. Routledge.

Harris, A., & Kuchuck, S. (Eds.). (2014). *The legacy of Sandor Ferenczi: From ghost to ancestor*. Routledge.

Hoffman, I. Z. (1991). Discussion: Toward a social-constructivist view of the psychoanalytic situation. *Psychoanalytic Dialogues, 1*(1), 74–105.

Kieffer, C. C. (2008). On siblings: Mutual regulation and mutual recognition. *Annals of Psychoanalysis, 36*, 161–173.

Kuchuck, S. (Ed.). (2014). Clinical implications of the psychoanalyst's life experience: When the personal becomes professional. Routledge.

Legorreta, G., Levaque, C., & Levinsky-Wohl, M. (2013). The sibling complex: Introduction and background. *Canadian Journal of Psychoanalysis, 21*(1), 170–174.

Levenson, E. A. (2009). The enigma of the transference. *Contemporary Psychoanalysis, 45*(2), 163–178.

Mitchell, J. (2003). *Siblings: Sex & violence*. Polity Press.

Mitchell, J. (2013). Siblings: Thinking theory. *Psychoanalytic Studies of the Child, 67*, 14–34.

Mitchell, S. (1988). *Relational concepts in psychoanalysis*. Harvard University Press.

Mitchell, S., & Aron, L. (Eds.). (1999). *Relational psychoanalysis: The emergence of a tradition*. Routledge.

Ogden, T. H. (1989). *The primitive edge of experience*. Jason Aronson.

Ogden, T. H. (1994). The analytic third: Working with intersubjective clinical facts. *International Journal of Psycho-Analysis, 75*, 3–19.

O'Leary, J., & Gaziano, C. (2011). Sibling grief after perinatal loss. *Journal of Prenatal & Perinatal Psychology and Health, 25*(3), 172–193.

Orange, D. (2014). Out of time: Siblings as trauma transmitters, protectors, sources of courage: Meeting Ron Bodansky's protest. *Psychoanalytic Inquiry, 34*(3), 251–261. https://doi.org/ 10.1080/07351690.2014.889482

Pizer, S. A. (1992). The negotiation of paradox in the analytic process. *Psychoanalytic Dialogues, 2*(2), 215–240.

Pollock, G. H. (1986). Childhood sibling loss: A family tragedy. *The Annual of Psychoanalysis, 14*, 5–34.

Rosner, S. (1985). On the place of siblings in psychoanalysis. *Psychoanalytic Review, 72*(3), 457–477.

Ruiz, G. (2012). Siblings, identity development and clinical process. *Journal of the American Psychoanalytical Association, 60*(6), 1289–1295.

Safer, J. (2002). *The normal one: Life with a difficult or damaged sibling.* The Free Press.

Siegel, D. J. (1999). *The developing mind: How relationships and the brain interact to shape who we are.* Guilford Press.

Silverman, S. (2006). Where we both have lived. *Psychoanalytic Dialogues, 16*(5), 527–542.

Solomon, A. (2012). *Far from the tree: Parents, children and the search for identity* (1st Scribner hardcover ed.). Scribner.

Solomon, A. (2019, September 2) The dignity of disabled lives. *The New York Times.*

Stern, D. B. (1983). Unformulated experience: From familiar chaos to creative disorder. *Contemporary Psychoanalysis, 19*, 71–99.

Stolorow, R., & Atwood, G. (2002). *Contexts of being: The intersubjective foundations of psychological life.* Routledge.

Sullivan, H. S. (1954). *The psychiatric interview.* W. W. Norton & Company.

Van der Hart, O., Nijenhuis, E., & Steele, K. (2006). *The haunted self: Structural dissociation and the treatment of chronic traumatization.* W. W. Norton & Company.

Vivona, J. M. (2010). Siblings, transference, and the lateral dimension of psychic life. *Psychoanalytic Psychology, 27*(1), 8–26. https://doi.org/10.1037/a0018637

Winnicott, D. W. (1974). Fear of breakdown. *International Review of Psycho-Analysis, 1*(1–2), 103–107.

Chapter 2

Sibling to sibling

Co-constructing our subjectivities in dialogue

Introduction: finding resonance

There is no expiration date to an experience not encountered in an embodied, integrated sense. Remarkably, it always remains there to be felt and found, this unexperienced-experience. The first thing that strikes me while interviewing people for the book is the recognition of there always being *more* to face in one's history of growing up alongside a disabled sibling. The external events happen/ed, but the absence of any space to inhabit and elaborate on their inner meanings remains ongoing as the disintegration between psyche, soma, and mind continue to split the experience into manageable parts. One of the adaptive features of dissociation is just that – it preserves experience in a safe house, stowed away from the day-to-day machinations of the waking "me." But under the right relational contexts, when developmental conditions are satisfied and a foundation of safety exists, the experience remains there to be both inhabited and encountered.

Bromberg (2008a, 2008b, 2008c) identifies the "experiential relational context" as a necessary precursor to the possibility of symbolizing dissociated content. Dissociated content is without linguistic representation but the right environment offers possibilities for formulation (Stern, 2004). But what makes a relational context experientially "right"? For this, I turn to developmental neuroscientist Dan Siegel (1999), who theorizes that coherent integration of experience within self-states is at the heart of human identity. For Siegel, resonance is an essential condition of a facilitative environment; he writes, "Integration involves the recruitment of internal and interpersonal processes into a mutually activating co-regulation" (1999, p. 321). Mutually activating implies the presence of an *other*. I read this to include both one's inner, well-resourced self-states, as well as actual other people outside the self-system. But not just any other state (of mind) or person will do. The features of the other must include someone or someplace within that can stand to be activated and utilize being activated affectively, in order to move what might otherwise become a nonreflective encounter (as in capital "E" enactment) into a reencountering, integrative experiential event. In analytic terms, this "other" must have the capacity to maintain or reestablish the analytic third for an enactment to yield experientially integrative features (Benjamin, 1990; Davies, 2004). Otherwise, where a transformative experience might have been, there is only repetition. I am trying to hone in on the part past repetition, to better examine the process of "working through" that I think Freud was getting at in his seminal idea of repetition as avoidance to remembering (Freud, 1914). What conditions facilitate reencountering and entering into unexperienced-experience? How do we re/acquire, or acquire for the first time, a license to own our own traumatic experience?

Dialoguing with other survivor siblings birthed possibilities for an inhabiting experience that I could not have imagined, and for which language will necessarily be limiting in describing. Practically every single interview at varying points throughout, either I or the subject, or us both together, would find ourselves often affectively saturated, welling up with tears, laughter, or anger that spilled forth a new capacity to *feel* something about the past *together* – something that had not until this very moment been felt as belonging to me/mine/ours, despite the sense of it having been there all along. This is what I mean by unexperienced-experience. It's not just a thought or unconscious fantasy – it's an experience that happened without an embodied witness or relational context with resonant presence. It may have previously existed in thought, or it may have been felt without thought or just encoded as a sensory experience without elaboration. Talking together brought forth a facilitative relational context as we connected, survivor sibling to survivor sibling. I could feel us begin to inhabit our thoughts, feelings, and memories into a living dialogue between us. The resonance facilitated inhabiting unexperienced-experience and working through. In this chapter, I aspire to convey how the sibling-to-sibling dimension was therapeutically useful in dissolving dissociative structure around the experience of survivorship.

Inhabiting my own activation

When I set out to write this book, I imagined that hearing from other analysts would illuminate aspects of survivorship that a memoir alone could not possibly account for. Because I was consciously interested in the impact of sibling survivorship on the clinical process, it felt important to include multiple perspectives. Perhaps I also needed others to be brave enough to go there in order to do so myself. What I did not expect, and could not predict, was that the data-gathering itself would become the most important part of this experience for me. I was not prepared – nor were my subjects – for the profound impact that talking sibling-to-sibling about an area of experience that has always been partially dissociated, historically not fully attended to, and profoundly othering brought forth. As one subject put it, *"after our first interview, I was left feeling, oh my God, you are the sister I always wanted!"*

Lest sharing this wishful statement makes it sound too rosy a picture, it was not immediately apparent that this outcome awaited me/us. After the first few interviews, I came to anticipate the following pattern in myself. Right before I'd call or open my door (some were remote, some were in person), my gut would tighten, and I'd feel dread, along with an inner monologue which began with *"why are you even doing this?"* My resistance to connecting with another regarding a legacy of survivorship was palatable and remained with me as a tightening in the belly and dryness in my throat. The words that often came to mind were *"self destructive"* and *"treasonous."* Sometimes it manifested somatically as I'd grow ill digestively just before a call, reliving an experience that would happen to me frequently as a kid. The dissociated content felt dangerous to unearth alone, never mind with another person who survived their own version of it, especially if I was supposed to be the one who I feared/imagined others hoped had something useful to "say" about it. It was not until the subject became a person in my office (or on a screen) that dread slipped below the surface. Anxiety of not making a fool of myself would propel me forward, as I'd introduce the structure for the interview. Anxiety being a great blocker for dread, I'd lose touch with the acute fear preceding it as I would click into a different state of survival mode.

This sequence repeated for me what it felt like to grow up alongside my severely disabled brother and initially (re)enacted the very thing I was there to learn about: fright, wreaking havoc on the body as the mind tries to organize the event and turn it into performance, with only a small hope of feeling connected and real – a tentative possibility perhaps located in some future time. After asking the initial question, which was always the same for each interview, I'd settle into a more contemplative and consultative position.

But what exactly was I dreading? Feeling these highly contradictory, emotionally charged memories and experiences? Experiencing the past as viscerally present in explicitly linking the psychic imprint of this autobiographical experience on my identity and life, breaking the taboo against knowing, alongside a fellow survivor? Naming the moral ambiguities around what makes life livable, at what expense, and who decides? Or was it feeling the pull of (dis)/loyalties to parents and the family narrative that frightened me most? My dread would spiral out to imagining the disability advocacy community coming to mock me for thinking we ordinary survivors needed some kind of special attention; this fantasy holding my shame about *having*. Each encounter offered either an opportunity to really be with these feelings and to come out on the other side changed for having felt them together; or what I feared even more, an opportunity to repeat the dissociative way of representing the experience, by having a heady conversation about the facts from the position of an observant bird – trading notes with one another high in the sky, but never really landing in the seat of this uncomfortable experience together.

There is no shortage of *as-if* experiences in the lives of survivor siblings who accommodate out of necessity, whatever their parent's defenses around chronic disability/illness brought forth (Winnicott, 1965). There is great difficultly utilizing fantasy in the service of imaginative strivings, as this realm is often replaced with a radically impossible pseudo-acceptance of what is. The limitations of the sibling's condition, its chronicity, the parent's unending reactivity or grief about it in whatever form it takes, and whether the disabled sibling grows up in the family home or in an institution, all constrain the full expression of what may be inside a survivor sibling's psyche. So much life/death experience happens without a mediated space in which to integrate it. I was terrified of becoming someone who contributed further to the already too large pool of as-if experience accumulated in my own and their imagined lives.

And yet, the camaraderie of this shared space began to feel to me like what I imagine veterans feel in proximity to one another. They know something about the ugliness of what surviving costs you, the carrying of the duplicity of surface gratitude at life alongside the undercurrent of other secret selves, whose identities and perspectives wholly differ from what may be seen outside. Once I sat with the intensity of these feelings in myself, I could come to recognize how being an insider gave me some home advantage. I worked hard to calm myself physically and emotionally while encountering this activation. I began to notice how the uncensored self (or less-censored self) is able to speak plainly without the same degree of fear that speaking to the uninitiated invites. Details aren't spared in the service of protecting the other's imagined reality. One interviewee remarked,

> *I was a graduate student when my (disabled) sister ultimately died. My advisor, who was a very sincere person, expressed the kind of sympathy you would imagine for the loss of non-disabled sibling, and I just felt so weird accepting it because it was not that, but she had no way of knowing how it was different for me. She just couldn't imagine it.*

It is not comfortable or easy to remain open to unsymbolized traumatic experience, but doing so creates the right experiential context for inhabitation to begin. Some of the things I could learn from having and sharing an insider perspective within the context of this dialogic process included the following sorts of "treasonous" feelings:

> *I always want/ed a sibling without a disability.*
> *I feared I'd be gotten rid of too.*
> *I resented and admired how much my parent (or parents) had to give to my disabled sibling that was not available to me.*
> *I wanted my sibling to go away or to never have been born.*
> *I never wanted my sibling to go away and could not bear the idea of their not having existed as this left me feeling like a murderer.*
> *My parents could have done a better job understanding me and my experience.*
> *I find little comfort in the company of my other non-disabled siblings.*
> *My siblings physical and/or emotional presentation disgusted, shamed, and embarrassed me.*
> *I miss a person that never existed.*

The intersubjective context of otherness

There can be so much shame in surviving something one's counterpart was not spared that evading annihilation anxiety can easily become a life's errand. I am indebted to each of the participants for being willing to "go there" with me, initially a virtual stranger to all but one of them.[1] The intersubjective context in which the interviews were conducted included my sharing two crucial identities with each of the participants – that of psychoanalyst and that of survivor sibling. Frie and Reis (2001) write:

> For the intersubjectivist, the subjectivity of the analyst is not just "in the room" with the patient's, it is in the world with the patient, as an irreducible other for whom considerations of recognition, ethics, dialogue, history, mutual influence, and creation are always already either being attended to or not.
>
> (p. 324)

I strove to attend to the unique shared intersubjective context. I participated in the interviews themselves promoting a sibling-transference/countertransference experience. I obtained consent to elaborate, react, and share my associations with what subjects relayed throughout the interview, creating an environment of mutual influence from the start. Rather than just ask the questions, an atmosphere of co-participation was present where I welcomed their questions of my experience as readily as I asked them about theirs. It could be felt within each dyadic encounter as we got lost in the experience of talking together, like siblings pulling for any input, elaboration, and contact the other might offer around this major life experience. The power to influence one another was bidirectional and existed *between* us in the interaction, as opposed to an authority that solely rested with me as the interviewer. Given the shared intersubjective context, the talking itself came to feel like a lateral rebellion of the vertical prohibition of silence that surrounds so much of family life. Finally, it seemed, there was a mediated presence where there had been none before.

This mutual resonance promoted by the sibling transference/countertransference field provided the right frame for unexperienced-experience of survivorship to be inhabited. Grossmark (2017) writes, "Meaning does not exist such that it can be interpreted, but rather comes into being through enactment itself, through dialogue and intersubjective engagement" (p. 32). Enacting my own vulnerability and revealing my own dissociative process, invited participants to do the same. The human experience contains somatic, behavioral, cognitive, sensorial, and procedural elements. In order to illustrate how unexperienced-experience became formulated between us, I will turn to parts of the interviews themselves and give examples of how this process worked along affective, behavioral, procedural, somatic, and cognitive lines. I do not mean to imply that things are integrated in categorical parts, but I have elected to organize the material this way for ease of relaying examples.

Part two: encountering unexperienced-experience

Affective derivative: close titration of hope/hopefulness

If there is an abundance of negative affect consistent with experiences of survivorship within the trauma spectrum, there is also guardedness around positive affect (Shapiro, 2018). An abiding sense of mistrust often pervades feeling good or hopeful, as it would have been reckless to live feeling hopeful that things would change as a child. The hopelessness may be stored in realms of unexperienced-experience and in adulthood may be dissociated from its autobiographical origins. In greeting **Rachel** for our second call to complete the interview, she asked after my son, and I replied,

> *I feel we hit the jackpot, he is just so loving and kind and interesting. It's not like I don't have adjustments and hard times, but I can't get over how wonderful an experience I am having and how much I love being with him. I'm waiting for the other shoe to drop.*

Rachel, a mom of three and colleague whom I knew prior to her participation in this study, gave me a kind, knowing smile. It was not until much later in the interview when she was telling me about her emotional experience of patients growing, that she said,

> *At first, I am often elated but then I don't trust it. You know? Like somewhere in the back of my mind, I'm always waiting for the other shoe to drop.*

I immediately heard myself back in her response and called our mutual attention to this mirror image. Was it more than coincidental for us to call on the same clichéd expression to capture the sensation of holding one's breath through life's positive moments? In a moment of moving connectivity and resonance, we felt together our sorrow for the one who holds her breath. Obsessional efforts to get ahead of loss complicate and contaminate hope. Survivor siblings may titrate their optimism, hope, and joy, initially out of necessity in accommodating the mixed reality of ambiguous loss as children – not dead, but not like-me – but ultimately out of habit. Titrating hope through the anticipation of dread gives oneself an illusion of safety, a safeguard as old as anxiety itself, which is to say if you expect it coming, it hurts less. But I was also left wondering, if we adopt the premise that none of us survivor siblings had yet fully experienced the inhibition around hope as it was housed within a dissociative state, Winnicott (1974) would say what we feared coming already came; and the more we pulled away at the cobwebs burying the initial shock of our sibling's disability and the attendant self-states generated by this reality, the less we would perhaps need to imagine it as the next thing around the bend. Talking with **Rachel** sensitized me to survivor siblings' difficulty sustaining and maintaining a relationship to hope. As a result, it became easier to notice how survivor siblings would locate hope (and the birth of new experience) elsewhere, as the next sequence of communication illustrates.

Harold had a severely physically and intellectually disabled younger brother by two years, whom he described as being unable to,

speak but he emoted in other ways, so there was no interaction with him on the subject of his challenges. I spent quite a lot of time going with my mom and brother to doctors' offices, clinics (not that it was ever explained why we were making those visits), but I intuited that it had to do with his slow and non-existing developmental progress.

Harold paints a vivid scene in which it's easy to imagine why being hopeful would feel assaultive to him as a young child, as each passing day brought further confirmation of his brother's limitations as well as a profound limit in his parent's capacity to translate what this might have felt like to **Harold**. The notable absence of any verbal dialogue surrounding his brother's condition within his family left him reaching affect saturation in talking so openly with me. As he spoke and responded to my questions, he gradually grew full of unprocessed affect.

Harold: I've always had such a creepy lonely feeling about family gatherings, they accentuate absence for me.

Me: I can see and feel how I am asking a lot of you to go back here. I've learned that it can be helpful when I share parts of my experience in these interviews. I'm not sure why this is coming to mind now, but my first dream in the only analysis that truly addressed my experience of survivorship took the form of finding my lost childhood dog. She had been missing and I had been looking and looking and looking for her, and in the dream suddenly there she was, in my backyard . . . all along.

Harold: That's really funny because you know what? I had a dog dream early in analysis too, which I actually see as a kind of liberation dream! My grandparents, in whose home I lived much earlier in life, had kind of a spooky cellar that I spent time in where my Grandpa would repair things . . . But alongside the house there was a very narrow . . . pathway, to the backyard that one got to by way of the cellar . . . In the dream, my grandparents dog, called Beauty, runs very freely and carelessly, not worried about this narrow passageway from the cellar, out into the yard, very exuberantly

Me: Right outside and into life?

Harold: Yeah, yes.

Me: As a beautiful one? Wow. I guess there's some resonance here in feeling our wish to reclaim what was lost to us. Family dogs are creatures that by nature get to honor their instincts more deliberately than we humans do. They look for freedom and are uninhibited in the grace of their movement. They can move through scary places. How funny that we both dreamt some version of this, and got here in talking today.

Harold: Yes. You know, I have a lot of betrayal issues related to the ways in which my parents didn't communicate with me.

The process itself cannot convey the change in the affective environment between us as it happened. It went from a feeling of imminent trauma saturation to one of connection through my trusting that what came to my mind would provide the right kind of relational resonance. Of course, I did not know it would also be a point of precise identification! That was an uncanny surprise. After this moment, it felt less like I was asking him to engage in an overwhelming process in which an "expert" sought information from a participant, and more like we were feeling our way into the difficulties around psychic liberation together as siblings, drawing on the same symbol. I believe these dreams at the beginning of treatment represented a buried hopefulness for the selves being found through the analytic process. As with **Rachel**, the hope is there, but it's hidden. This made it possible for him to continue inhabiting his experience, as he moved on toward talking about how feeling betrayed by his parents left him dissociated from his own experience. In talking together, we conjured up a mutual wish for the freedom to explore and to roam the terrain in which this legacy had been lived. This freedom cannot be found unless one bears a capacity to move unexperienced-experience into the realm of embodiment. An important component of doing so requires the facilitative environment of resonance between subjects.

Behavioral derivative: commitment to serving the other/unrepresented

As I understand it historically, psychoanalysis has not conceived of behavior as a useful portal into unconscious experience and instead tended to criticize patients for "acting out" their unconscious, instead of following the rule of moving the action into language. The object relational movement ushered in new ways of conceiving of action symbolically and not simply from a place of a patient's "resistance" or poor impulse control, extending contemporarily to a fine appreciation of the analyst's own use of action as a means of interpretation (Ogden, 1994). When it comes to dissociated material, much of what remains outside awareness must first gain recognition through behavioral enactments and so thankfully the taboo on working with or noticing behavior is no longer with us from the one-person framework of acting out or resistance. Instead of resistance, behavioral eruptions are treated as (unconscious) communications. Stern (2004) defines enactment as "the interpersonalization of dissociation" (p. 213) to capture the duality and embedded co-occurring nature of both the analyst and the patient's (dissociative not-me) contributions coming into contact. There is a growing appreciation of this phenomenon, including Ogden's (1979, 1994) interpretation through action and his thinking about projective identification as a communication, Levenson's (1988) premise of the dream-telling re-creating the dream scene, and Stern's (2004) philosophy of moving dissociated content between people into intrapsychic conflict within them via enactment among others. Grossmark broadens the notion of behavioral enactments to include that which happened but also that which is "yet to be experienced and symbolized, and also enactments of what has never happened, or of what was lacking, such as the consequences of neglect" (p. 28).

The analytic context facilitates the translation of unconscious experience embedded within the behavior. But broadly speaking, we are always enacting our unconscious in all contexts, "Attuning ourselves to the phenomenon of enactment suggests an emerging participatory awareness . . . [but] enactive process is by no means restricted to the therapeutic situation" (Brown, 2020, p. 76). What is the fate of enactments that occur outside the analytic context? This is the question that guided me as I listened to interviewees describe their involvement in issues related to social justice.

Many survivor siblings were in touch with a sense of pride about championing the rights of marginalized groups and identified these efforts as a strong defining feature in their sense of self. The behaviors around advocacy held lots of enactive process around the unconscious correlate of having one's own direct or indirect experience of marginalization (located in external reality vis-à-vis their sibling and/or an awareness of parts of self that felt impoverished and neglected). Many interviewees described the lived inheritance of an anti-bias perspective vis-à-vis their exposure and proximity to disability within their familial situation. Another realm of unexperienced-experience that sharpened under the lens of our interaction included how this advocacy, seemingly on behalf of the voiceless sibling, was underlying and representing the voiceless agonies of the survivor siblings' own split self-states. Advocacy was as much tied with the representation of the sibling as it was with the inner buried needs of certain self-states, as themes of family separation and trauma permeate the cultural milieu of our contemporary surround. As we got talking, the enactive elements within this behavior came into focus.

Susan, a mid-aged female analyst, tells me about the events surrounding the birth of her disabled younger sister and her mother's subsequent psychiatric hospitalization from the perspective of her seven-year-old self, "*Mom went away to get help to stop the crying.*" **Susan** relays memories of getting into trouble, often with authority figures in school. But it was not until our interview that she linked this troublesomeness, what she coined her contrarian personality and her current commitment to being a social justice agitator, to the family situation:

Susan: I was four when my disabled sister was born. And I have memories of my Mom disappearing going to the hospital and coming back with a baby and it seemed to be fine and normal, I guess from my perspective as a 5 year old . . . but my sister did not develop normally, it was like we had an infant around for two years. I remember having a mix of pride that I'm a very needed person in the family and also resenting it, coming home from school everyday to do this. I was an angry kid . . . when my mom was hospitalized, I was, as a first grader, suspended repeatedly for misbehaving and being enraged with my teacher, who I think was probably less than understanding and compassionate. I remember one day taking off my hard solid oxford shoes and throwing them at her, and I was sent back to Kindergarten as a punishment.

Me: Sent *back?* How cruel an intervention given the circumstances of your sister's lack of development and your mother's absence?

Susan: Yea. A lot of punishment, but you know, I didn't connect the anger at school with what was happening at home. Maybe I was always disrupting boundaries in places that I felt were very unfair. It's helping me right now to formulate that; it makes so much sense when I look at my adult life now, as I continue to disrupt boundaries in the service of social justice.

Me: I've found it useful to share my associations as we go, and a memory from college is what comes to mind. In this creative writing class we had to share a poem we'd written aloud, and I wrote a poem in which I described my experience of finding my disabled brother at the bottom of the staircase in our family home. He is paraplegic, he has no control over his musculature, the poem was just a description of my view of him, actually from the top of the stairs, and so the poem I guess, was very sad about how I could get up and down those stairs and he couldn't. For the peer review, you weren't allowed to say what the poem was about before the class responded, and it was just inconceivable to the students to figure out the meaning of my work. It turned into some perverse guessing game. They guessed it was a doll, they guessed it was about my separating from a doll, and I remember holding in tears because I hadn't set out to write this, I had never really written about it before, it just poured out of me. I didn't know where it came from or what it meant to be sharing these feelings, but the misrecognition and the fact that in no one's imagination could this have been a human being, let alone a relative of mine, was just stunning. A kind of prejudice enacted through absence of contemplating the existence of an other, a disabled other. Not even like I am against you, but I can't even conceive of you!

Susan: Yes, exactly. That has been a part of my commitment to social justice, heightening awareness, bringing knowledge of otherness into consciousness. It's one of the things I have gotten from my experience with my sister. My parents really battled the medical community who said to institutionalize my sister whose life expectancy was 5. They said institutionalize her and my parents said, *"no no we won't, we won't."* And I guess, it had a huge impact on the family – but they conveyed to us, she was us.

Something sharpens and clicks into focus for us both about this commitment to reaching others in extremis, including our own dissociated, traumatized selves in these gestures. As the interview progresses, **Susan** calls attention to how my questions lean toward what is lost, as opposed to what is gained, by having a family organized around the advocacy of a disabled family member. She is not alone in representing this position.

Darlene talks of being very involved in political advocacy for immigrant families who have been forcibly separated under the current presidential administration. She likens this experience to her sister's institutionalization and the sense of powerlessness she felt at the time, which turned into an urgent need to give her sister a voice, or to give voice to the voiceless, and to keep families together. Buried underneath and unconsciously there is the wish to save oneself from loss, even though the behavior appears to be directed toward and for the "other." As she tells me this, her passion floods the line and I can feel she means what she says.

But arguably there is a quality of psychic equivalence in this mode, in which all separations harken back to the actual and intrapsychic personal one/s (Fonagy et al., 2002). This legacy of survivorship impels the soul forward on the course to rescue others, actual and fantasized, from the fate one has lived. The outcome may well be one that drives social justice efforts forward in the collective, but from a psychic developmental perspective, it takes linking these behaviors with one's own unexperienced-experience to integrate the particular meanings held within the behavioral dimension. Talking together seemed to move unconsciously motivated actions around advocacy into the realm of consciousness, dissolving dissociative structures within the survivor sibling as these links and points of identification were explicitly noticed and made between us.

Process derivative: repetition of silence

More on the salience of silence will follow in the next chapter, but here I want to highlight how in talking together, participants and I disrupted and encountered the silence of unformulated silos in our own process, our parent's process, and our imagined disabled sibling's process. **Carolyn,** the second eldest in a lineup of four siblings whose youngest sister is severely disabled, tells me:

So the story we were told, we were told right away, was that something had gone wrong at birth and they weren't sure if she was going to live . . . I don't remember a time when I didn't know something was wrong . . . I shared this identification with her readily . . . I was a preemie baby, and she was preemie, so I identified with her needing some special care in the beginning.

She went on to tell me how her father conveyed his grief and fear, but that her Mom is "harder to interpret":

On the one hand she has been the primary caretaker but emotionally much more detached. I think she was depressed as well, but she never really talks about it, what it was like for her that her baby had this issue, that she almost died. There wasn't a feeling about it from my mom, other than devotion and duty and dedication to her care. And I was initially over-identified, but quietly so, with my sister in her needs for maternal care.

Carolyn was very responsive when I conveyed my impression that what comes across in each of these encounters is the interpersonal silence surrounding the experience and how this inhibits internal elaborations. Even when siblings are given some stories or information about what may be happening – and for many of us this is an *if* – the field feels affectively closed in terms of families being able to talk to each other about it while remaining *experientially* present. So much gets communicated without direct discussion, leaving unconscious communication the primary mode of contact, or through behaviorally motivated discussions, like instilling a commitment to advocacy, incidentally crowding out the possibility for recognizing conflictual feelings and struggles. For example, often no one asks explicitly about who will assume caretaking responsibilities for the disabled sibling when the parents pass. I queried Carolyn about this:

Carolyn: Um, I feel like I have always known that it'd fall to me. It was not really made official until oh let's see, I don't know, probably around college.

Me: This project began with my flashbacks to my brother's midnight seizures and how this experience was lived – for me, my mom, my dad- my younger brother was not alive yet. It was like no one talked about it. We went through this intense experience but the next day, or years later, even now, the emotional part of it wasn't talked about. It was surreal in it's un-articulated state, very much felt but not there verbally and un-mentalized, so like what do children do? Where do they put it?

Carolyn: Yeah no one talked about the effect it had on the rest of us, the children. There was some talk about its impact on my disabled sibling and the quality of her life, and on my mom, but not on us and not directly.

Me: Yes, and for you in particular as the one who shared a room with her, and as you told me your sister's primary attachment figure and soother, wow. I can only imagine what that silence must have been like inside you.

Carolyn: Yeah, I mean that's kind of why, because it wasn't talked about, I could say to myself, ok mom is too tired and out of resources for herself and all I could feel was my sister's need to be calmed down, and mine too and it just became inevitable, ok I'm going to have to do this. Which of course I couldn't do, but I mean, in a lot of ways I did. But it was a struggle every time.

This initial silence coupled with the failure to imagine the survivor's internal experience was re-encountered as she later relays that:

In 10 years of psychoanalytic therapy these experiences never came up, and it still amazes me that this was never a serious topic in my work in the therapy! And oddly I knew my analyst had a son that had a disability; it wasn't as severe as my sister's. But I never put that together either, until now in our talking, that my analyst and I may have been repeating the silence. I don't think we talk about siblings enough anyway as a real relationship that's just as significant as our parents, let alone a sibling like ours, whose presence changes life in so many ways. That just wasn't something people talked about.

The configuration of silence surrounding **Rose's** family was different from **Carolyn's** but nonetheless pivotal in informing the dissociative content of unexperienced-experience. **Rose** had a severely disabled sister 2.5 years older than her, who was put in an institutional setting in toddlerhood. **Rose** believes that her parents' marriage deteriorated over their differing feelings about institutionalizing her sibling when she was 3 years old.

I think they were not emotionally equipped people, and so they didn't have the strongest relationship to begin with, but with the birth of my sister it broke them. There was just no discussion. The relationship ended. I am aware that it's hard for me to talk about this stuff right now.

When I query her about what she knows about why it's hard to talk right now, her response surprises me:

Actually my family is here visiting, in the other room, so it might be better because in a lot of ways, this recreates what it was like!

I suddenly realize that she is crouched down on the floor of her bedroom, laptop on her lap, with her door closed and that her soft tone is intentional, to avoid being overheard. This semi-conspiratorial tone permeated the rest of our interview, as if we were literally two siblings in a closet discussing these feelings that were otherwise unshared and unspoken about with the remaining family just outside her door. She noted how their proximity and her secretiveness re-created the conditions surrounding her childhood experience of her disabled sister, and the family situation, actually making it easier for her to encounter this unexperienced-experience as it re-presented itself in real time. Part of that included feeling the sadness that the secrecy demanded of us in dialogue together. On the other side of silence, there was a lot of pain.

It just wasn't talked about. I never felt brave enough to bring it up. Few times I asked about my sister, my mom would cry, I don't really remember. But I was extremely tuned in to my mom, on her well being and needing her to know that I was ok. It's been hard to understand how I'm feeling throughout my life because there was no help in that department.

In another instance, **Debra**, an astute observer of the process, reflected with me on how prior treatments somehow sustained the silence around her experience of her disabled sibling as opposed to disrupting it.

Debra: Well, I entered therapy any number of times trying to work something out and would inevitably need to go back. Something was missing. But it wasn't until my training analysis with the person I ended up with, who from the very start kept hearing references to my sister! I mean apart from the comfort of realizing, wow some stuff happened to me, he consistently heard these references to her.

Me: I understand what that's like. I had many prior therapies where the dissociation around this experience was enacted but never translated and it left me feeling alien-like. It was another 4 years in the right treatment before I had room to imagine who my disabled brother might have been, were he not profoundly disabled for the first time ever. I had never had the room or process to imagine this. The silence surrounded the experience so fully it killed off any chance of imagining or of the other person noticing.

Debra: There is something about talking to someone who's experience, though different than mine, still has so many similarities. There is something so wildly illuminating, sharing this experience that is incredibly hard to describe to someone that either doesn't have an analytic background or a disabled person in their lives, but you have both. Even people who absolutely love me, and I have no doubt of their love for me, can't see these wounds. And as you were speaking I was just really moved by this process. There is something about the word profound that you used to describe your brother's condition that was itself profound. An acknowledgment. Of what holding this experience is like.

Somatic derivative: storing traumatic memory in the body

Psychoanalysts are indebted to pioneers in the field of Trauma Studies for advancing a humanitarian, psyche-soma perspective that considers the effects of trauma on human development (Ogden et al., 2006; Shapiro & Forrest, 1997; Siegel, 1999; Van der Hart et al., 2006; Van Der Kolk, 2014). We'd be remiss not to consider the impact on the body of this unexperienced-experience, which I noted earlier in my own process of conducting these interviews as I detailed my own activation. It was first my body, then the hyper-aroused thoughts of fight, flight, or fake it that followed in approaching this content. Chefetz (2015) describes how dissociative content can be stored in the somatosensory associations of the body, and in *The Body Keeps the Score*, Van Der Kolk (2014) also writes:

> The body keeps the score: If the memory of trauma is encoded in the viscera, in heartbreaking and gut-wrenching emotions, in autoimmune disorders and skeletal/muscular problems, and if mind/brain/visceral communication is the royal road to emotion regulation, this demands a radical shift in our therapeutic assumptions.
>
> (p. 88)

But what conditions of safety are necessary for a survivor sibling to approach their sensory experience with openness? Is resonance alone enough? If trauma disrupts the mind-body connection, all incoming data from the body is experienced by the mind as threatening. If self-regulation is the way back to psyche-soma integration, and by definition is lacking for survivor siblings, how might mutual regulation facilitate a body-based awareness? How might we translate these bodily experiences into a kind of *knowing*?

Olina, the oldest of three siblings, two of whom have disabilities, tells me about her memory of the birth of her youngest brother who has Down syndrome.

Olina: I was probably four when he was born, so still not old enough to have a lot of clear memory. I think it was probably traumatizing, he was born so early.

Me: How early*?*

Olina: *(anxiousness or an excess of emotion floods her voice)* You know I don't remember, these are all good questions, I wish I knew.

Me: I think most people when they come to this question think, well this is what I know, but in the retelling of what is known, we all discover the holes and the remaining questions. It's like, well if it didn't involve evoking parent's pain and vulnerabilities, you might know more or have felt able to ask it later on. It's tricky. So he came early, you're not sure how early?

Olina: Yes, I don't want to upset my parent's more. I know his esophagus was not connected partially up to the stomach, there was no connection, which posed an immediate risk to his life so he had surgery as an infant *(begins crying)*. He was in the hospital for the first 100 days of his life. It's surprising I'm getting so emotional now, but I don't talk about it all the time. *(Interviewer begins to cry too)*. I'm now more just imagining what that's like because I don't remember it really. My parents would get calls overnight to come when they thought he wasn't going to make it. A lot of other family must have stepped in to take care of us. I do remember being very excited when he was finally coming home, I don't have a visual memory of it, but the feeling is there in my body, but we knew that from the beginning, he had Down syndrome.

Me: Where do you feel it in your body?

Olina: My solar plexus area.

Me: Whether it's talked about or not may be a misleading way of getting at this question because even if it is talked about, it can't possibly be talked about in a way that attends to the full experience as it's happening. That's something I am noticing as we talk together now.

Olina: Yeah, it's just like there's not even words for it. You know, I am actually getting a certification in body training. I learned there is so little containment in my solar plexus, I just give it all away.

Me: Maybe part of the psychic compensation for being able-bodied is to not really know, to not really be in touch with the body, to hold the body back, but I also think there is some interesting relationship between the autoimmune disorders, or IBS, and the survivor sibling experience. At least, there is for me. Trauma takes its toll.

Olina: Totally, that's why I initially sought therapy. I started having IBS symptoms in college, and my first therapist wasn't wonderful but I finally had some help. And my parents whose insurance I was using to get the treatment at some point said, "I don't think you really need this anymore," and I was like "yeah, you're right," because my IBS was better controlled at the time, but inside I was just devastated. Because *(crying)* I was in pain. There needed to be some physical permission, some body experience, to validate my getting this kind of care and even then, it was subject to interruption.

In another interview **Hannah**, who is the twin to a brother with severe Cerebral Palsy, shared this reflection:

Hannah: Bodies for a long time represented my brother's disabled body. While I never explicitly related it to my experience of his body, talking with you now is making me aware of how this impacted my relationship to my own body. It was always, "I have to get out of here." I never really related to my body, it was just this thing I had to drag around to clothe and feed it. I dissociate very easily, it was my go-to for when things were too hard to take in and on.

Me: Yes, I'm so glad you are making these connections now because most interviewees first go to their ego or their mind's experience of the sibling's condition/parent's reactions, but you stand out for going right to the absence of body, right into the somatic experience of dissociation. Or the extreme linking of your physicality with your disabled twin siblings, as if the connection could be fostered between you by what was felt in your body as belonging to him. But that you did not have an experience of your body separate from his, or what you experience as his sensations?

Hannah: Exactly. I still remember, the first time I ever encountered a body as beautiful was when I saw an Olympic gymnast, and their power and grace just hit me all at once, like propelled me back or for the first time really, into seeing bodies as having a capacity to be beautiful. I was a young adult. This discussion clarifies why bodies in space have been so absorbing and interesting to me all these years. It must continue to inform me in ways I don't even know and am still learning about!

Cognitive derivative: reawakening descriptive scenic memory

A final realm of unexperienced-experience that came into focus during the process of these dialogues was memory for details not described or elaborated on before. **Kira,** whose sister was born normally but at 17 months old, had a seizure that precipitated permanent and lifelong disability following a medical error at a routine doctor's visit, painted such a vibrant picture of her family life that I felt as if I stepped into her home and immediately recognized it. As she described her family pushing her sister's wheelchair down the aisles at church feeling a sense of righteousness that no one would call them out on their tardiness given the challenges of the reality they lived – and how that righteousness masked a profound shame beneath it – brought to mind memories of my disabled brother making sounds of affectation during quiet moments at synagogue. **Kira** then reminded me of another huge feature of family life:

We had twenty four hour nursing care through Medicaid. We became very close to our nurses, they came to our weddings, we still stay in touch with them.

It hit me – of course, the health aides! Who had become to feel a part of the family given the degree of their involvement in the intimacies of care-taking. **Kira** goes on to say:

As I got older I had to help care for my sister a lot when nurses would call out during holidays and snow storms. From a very young age I learned how to administer medications, check her oxygen tank, pick her up to put her in her wheelchair, like I probably should have been a nurse, but I didn't go there. We had a fully operating hospital in our house. I mean from high school, young high school, I'd stay up all night with my sister to give my parent's a break. I remember senior year, missing a party to give my mom a break.

As I listen to Kira, my mind is filled with scenic recollections of my child-hood home – the industrial-sized delivery box of adult-sized diapers that sat in the foyer of my house as my brother aged, the various wheelchairs with different colors and features, the black, white and red tiling of our handicap accessible bathroom, and the contractors my parents hired to make a wheelchair ramp entrance to the back door of our house. More images come: of my brother's hospital bed, which allows you to sit up or lay flat; the high-grade food processor, which was used to puree and pul-verize his food, as he could not chew. I'm overcome noticing the things all around that were always there and a part of the actual environment but not talked about or encountered in dialogue like this before. It's some version of a me-too moment. **Kira** continues,

Kira: A lot of my work in treatment focused on my sister's ultimate death, when I was pregnant myself with my first child. It was a year of firsts without her. The main aspect we had time to get to was my guilt. I had an obsession, I was drawn to my sister's grave, and we had a lot of snow that year, and I'd drive there with a shovel and shovel the snow off of her grave while I was pregnant, which was crazy. . .

Me: It's not crazy.

Kira brings her gaze to meet mine, and with surprised eyes that I imagine seem to register she has permission not to tell this story through a pathologizing lens, goes on to say in a softer, younger voice:

I was afraid she was cold. In fact, when we closed her casket, we put a blanket on her. It snowed a lot. I had a dream towards the end of my treatment with my therapist . . . I dreamt my sister was on the floor above me in the hospital where I worked. The whole day I was so busy, I never got to visit her. In the dream, I felt I had to get up there to comb her hair, but all day long I kept making excuses that there were patients I had to see. I couldn't just go up the stairs. Finally, I got there and my sister was sitting there smiling with her hair neatly braided and she was fine. She didn't need me. She was ok. And there was like no reason for my worry.

In talking with **Kira,** the details of a narrative memory began to take shape as a dissociative process regarding the environmental surroundings began to crumble for us both. Dissociative processes can be stored in inanimate objects as easily as other people. Seeing together the presence of health aides, the diapers, the blenders, and the medical paraphernalia, all coming into focus was as if we both regained a previously muted vision of our lives. As the early life became enlivened between us, **Kira** found her way to the penultimate loss of her sister. From a self-state perspective, her dream shows how her overfunctioning self is split apart from the vulnerable dependent one, so much so that by the time she goes to visit her, even the dependent one has found a way to survive on her own. The medical supplies, the aides, the environment so carefully crafted to the care of the disabled one, all rework the survivor sibling's psyche, inhibiting their vulnerability and pulling for their compensatory selves. But what happens to the survivor when they outlive the experience in which their survivorship has a purpose? How does a non-integrated self-system impact the future? As Chefetz (2015) so succinctly states, "dissociation is not so much of a problem until it refuses to give back, what it protectively takes: the liveliness of experience, the context and the meaning of what happens" (p. 25).

Conclusion: integration follows resonant experiential contact

Being present with our emotions, cognitions, sensorial experience, and memories offered a unique opportunity to inhabit together what had been for most of us, at best, only partially experienced absent space for mediation and reflection. Encountering this resonance sibling-to-sibling, healingly allowed me to more fully inhabit my own experience. The change carried over beyond my recollections of early survivorship experience and made me confront, in the present tense, old habituated ways I had maintained keeping those parts of (self) experience outside of my awareness. The courageousness of going "there" together became contagious. It brought forth new ways of being with what is happening now in the present and of fully attending to experience as it unfolds. Listening and speaking from a place of embodiment, and holding the conviction that it is never too late to encounter and encode throughout the psyche-soma this kind of dissociative content, can make a world of difference inside a survivor sibling's selves.

Note

1 A colleague I knew from a peer supervision group participated in the study.

References

Benjamin, J. (1990). Recognition and destruction: An outline of intersubjectivity. In S. A. Mitchell & L. Aron (Eds.), *Relational psychoanalysis* (pp. 32–60). The Analytic Press.

Bromberg, P. M. (2008a). "Grown-up" words: An interpersonal/relational perspective on unconscious fantasy. *Psychoanalytic Inquiry, 28*, 131–150.

Bromberg, P. M. (2008b). Mentalize THIS!: Dissociation, enactment, and clinical process. In E. Jurist, A. Slade, & S. Bergner (Eds.), *Mind to mind: Infant research, neuroscience, and psychoanalysis* (pp. 414–434). Other Press.

Bromberg, P. M. (2008c). Shrinking the tsunami: Affect-regulation, dissociation, and the shadow of the flood. *Contemporary Psychoanalysis, 44*, 329–350.

Brown, R. (2020). *Groundwork for a transpersonal psychoanalysis*. Routledge.

Chefetz, R. (2015). *Intensive psychotherapy for persistent dissociative processes: The fear of feeling real*. W. W. Norton Company.

Davies, J. (2004). Whose bad objects are we anyway? Repetition and our elusive love affair with evil. *Psychoanalytic Dialogue, 14*(6), 711–732.

Fonagy, P., Gergely, G., Jurist, E., & Target, M. (Eds.). (2002). *Affect regulation, mentalization, and the development of the self*. Other Press.

Freud, S. (1914). Remembering, repeating and working-through (Further recommendations on the technique of psycho-analysis II). In *The standard edition of the complete psychological works of Sigmund Freud, volume XII (1911–1913): The case of Schreber, papers on technique and other works* (pp. 145–156). London and Hogarth Press.

Frie, R., & Reis, B. (2001). Understanding intersubjectivity. *Contemporary Psychoanalysis, 37*(2), 297–327.

Grossmark, R. (2017). Narrating the unsayable: Enactment, repair, and creative multiplicity in group psychotherapy. *International Journal of Group Psychotherapy, 67*(1), 27–46.

Levenson, E. A. (1988). The pursuit of the particular. *Contemporary Psychoanalysis, 24*(1) 1–16.

Ogden, P., Minton, K., & Pain, C. (2006). *Trauma & the body: A sensorimotor approach to psychotherapy*. W. W. Norton & Company.

Ogden, T. H. (1979). On projective identification. *International Journal of Psycho-Analysis, 60*, 357–373.

Ogden, T. H. (1994). The concept of interpretive action. *The Psychoanalytic Quarterly, 63*(2), 219–245.

Shapiro, F. (2018). *Eye movement desensitization and reprocessing (EMDR) therapy* (3rd ed.). The Guilford Press.

Shapiro, F., & Forrest, M. S. (1997). *EMDR: Eye movement desensitization and reprocessing*. Basic Books.

Siegel, D. (1999). *The developing mind: How relationships and the brain interact to shape who we are*. Guilford Press.

Stern, D. (2004). The eye sees itself: Dissociation, enactment, and the achievement of conflict. *Contemporary Psychoanalysis, 40*(2), 197–237.

Van der Hart, O., Nijenhuis, E., & Steele, K. (2006). *The haunted self: Structural dissociation and the treatment of chronic traumatization*. W. W. Norton Company.

Van der Kolk, B. A. (2014). *The body keeps the score: Brain, mind, and body in the healing of trauma*. Viking.

Winnicott, D. W. (1965). *The maturational process and the facilitating environment: Studies in the theories of emotional development*. International Universities Press.

Winnicott, D. W. (1974). Fear of breakdown. *International Review of Psycho-Analysis, 1*, 103–107.

Chapter 3

The silent explosion

Impacts of early developmental experiences in survivorship

My brother, Teddy, was born with the umbilical cord wrapped around his neck. Cord compression occurred in utero so he was without oxygen for an unknown period of time before he made his way out of my mother's womb. My parents were told right away at birth that something was wrong with my brother. My mom had suspected something had gone suddenly wrong in her last days of pregnancy with him, but was persuaded by her obstetrician that she was understandably anxious given the twin stillbirth delivery she'd had before him. This critical part of the story explains so much of my mom to me: her intuition, ignored and written off as feminine hysteria, later came true. The extent and severity of my brother's disability would reveal itself over the course of his development. Doctors gave him a lifespan of no more than five years at birth.

Introduction

This chapter aims to locate the intrapsychic impressions left by the disabled sibling on the survivor sibling, as well as the interpersonal strategies of fomenting a relationship across the ability spectrum between siblings. It is hard for me to describe what it is like to seek out my brother without my mom's dissociated grief and concurrent manic attendant management strategies intruding on the space. I am not alone in this – all the interviewees I spoke to would try to tell me about their experience of their sibling and their sibling's condition, but always contextualize it within the parameters of what was made possible by the caregiver's framework and unconscious allowance. Searching for the survivor siblings "I's" in a sea of familial unprocessed affect is not easy to do.

My mother was an avid storyteller of the biographical kind. She wove threads of events through personable details lining them up in such a way to make us all pretty fantastic fiction. She was always creating characters and moral storylines out of our lives, her own included. What stands out most about these stories now was the amused tone in which they were told to me. On the surface she seemed charmed by her creations and her projections of my ingenuity, but to me as a listener, the incongruence between the events she described, how she sounded, and what I felt about them, were unsettling, not unlike the feeling of tinnitus in the ears that only you can hear – low grade, but there enough to cause some discomfort. Her amused quality left me feeling observed from afar and relationally required that I split my experience into parts in order to maintain the connection. During her storytelling, I'd experience myself as an object; a livable, smart, interesting object, but an object all the same (as opposed to a knowable subject), as the parts of my experience that she could not see or name or ask me about remained outside the vision of who I was. Objectification feels exploitative whether it has a negative or positive charge, and it contributes to a sense of unreality of being known/existing. This depersonalization accompanying the storytelling creates the conditions in which unexperienced-experience is stored. On the surface, it feels more confusing when objectification takes on a positive, idealized charge because it does not seem to be a "bad" thing. But no matter how cleverly my Mom would refashion her own dissociated subjectivity into a kind of family narrator pastime, I often felt lonely and missed her and myself, even when we were together. One such story that I was told by her throughout my childhood went like this:

When you were almost five years old, you came up to me and said, "Mommy, I swallowed something" *as you clutched your belly. I asked what you swallowed, and you pointed towards the laundry area, settling on the bottle of laundry detergent and complaining of a stomach-ache. You looked ill, and in a panic I dialed 9–11. As we rode to the ER in the ambulance, I watched your expression of pain turn into one of curiosity. By the time we reached the hospital in the examining room when the Attending doctor asked you what happened, the first thing you said was,* "Is this where Teddy goes when he comes here? Are you Teddy's doctor?".

The story ends with her taking me home from the hospital leaving her feeling both relieved that I was okay per physical examination, and amused that I had satiated my curiosity about the parts of my brother's experiences following his seizures that I did not see. Hearing the story, a visual memory of standing in front of the washer would come to mind, but that's the only part of it for which I have any memory – and whether that's my seeing *her story* or my memory, remains a little unclear to me. It's also unclear whether I actually swallowed something or if I only said I did, as the story implies. What has become clear to me is that her affect foreclosed a space I think I really needed. It anticipated how we should all feel about this scene, rather than invite a dialogue about what my experience of Teddy's disability and life-threatening seizures were like for me. As an adult, it left me with more questions than answers. Why would I have gone to such lengths to see where my brother was sent during the emergencies? What made it feel like something I could not ask about outright? What motivated me to seek injury – real or imagined, as I still do not know – in order to find my brother's experience? What did I imagine was happening to him there? How fearful was I about making my parents angry or sad that I went to legitimize and disguise my curiosity with this gesture? How come in the retelling, there is no moment of recognition in the parent or the doctor as in: *"Oh, is this young girl suffering from fear, uncertainty, jealousy, confusion around her brother's condition? How do we deal with it, and the attention it warrants?"* Could everyone really just believe that all I needed was to see the literal room Teddy visited, case closed?

As I write this now, another memory comes unbidden – this one wholly of my own recollection. Sometimes as a kid, I'd slip into bed with my older brother Teddy. I'd lie beside him, and tell him feelings I had that could not be acknowledged elsewhere. I'd pretend we were sharing stories back and forth, knowing my confessions were safe with him as he is nonverbal. I had some fantasy that he was containing and participating in connecting with me *like a real sibling*, conspiring in the dark and admitting our fears and desires. Somehow, in his bed as opposed to his wheelchair, it became easier to will an equal cognizant other, a reciprocal relation, into an imaginative existence. Without the diapers, wheelchair, handicapped accessible van, and various indicators of his disability that so obviously limited the degree to which he could participate reciprocally, when we were side-by-side in the dark, we were just a brother and a sister, and I could pretend that my impossible wish to connect in a mutual way on verbal ground, might be willed into existence. I was looking for him, trying to find him; missing him, though I lay right beside him.

The inner and outer landscape of survivor siblings

A survivor sibling is often left holding unnamed fears of contamination, mortality (of self and others), and catastrophic loss that sharpen with age and comprehension, alongside the guilt of surviving and being perceived as being more "intact." The incongruence between how others perceive the self and how the inner selves are experienced may result in real difficulties discerning truth from fiction. Chefetz (2015) writes, "Knowing about dissociative process means understanding that there is more to the structuring of experience than ideational content or linguistic narrative" (p. 24). Negotiating these experiences becomes a lifetime's work and often a lonely one for the survivor sibling. Mourning for the relationship that could never come into fruition with one's disabled sibling and missing something you never had gets buried underneath the anxiety and rage of surviving, and for some, this may remain within the realm of unexperienced-experience. What often complicates the picture is the difficulty in getting recognition/support for these feelings from caregivers, who are initially lost to the cause of caring for the disabled sibling and later wed to whatever defensive structure gets adopted for handling their own grief, consequently leaving them either very dissociated in particular about the impact the disabled sibling has on the psychic experience of the other children in the home, or more attentive to it, in a surface behavioral kind of way, as if they can insulate the survivor sibling from loss by making sure they still get to do "ordinary things."

The metaphor of a silent explosion seems to capture this well; something is immediately and irrevocably set off at the birth of the disabled sibling for which survivor siblings lack a coherent linguistic conceptualization. The silence is meant to capture how unsafe it feels to ask or to know what's happening, despite the obvious visual cues of the world having been blown up. The explosion into another dimension of reality unquestionably occurs without a helpful soundtrack to accompany it. Family life goes on around this explosion, creating an eerie sense of dislocation between the encountered destruction and the family narrative built up around it.

Theory interlude: the interpenetration of reality and fantasy

Whole schools of psychoanalytic thought have distinguished themselves on the basis of where they lay their emphasis, as in the intrapsychic/object relational approach, the self or the interpersonal school, each implicitly claiming they have closer access to unconscious process. A Relational approach does not position fantasy as more meaningful than our co-constructed reality, or even as something that resides as separate from it, as other analytic objectivist stances have been able to assume. Instead, Relational theorizing considers the always indeterminate, bidirectional, constantly occurring impact that our psychic life has on our actual relationships – fantasized and otherwise. There is, conceptually speaking, no longer a separate realm where the unconscious and our inner objects reside, but instead an unending blending of these intertwined dimensions of experience (Kuchuck & Sopher, 2017). Bonovitz (2010) describes how in health, the dialectical tension is held between fantasy and reality, with each dimension enriching the other; whereas in disturbance, one realm may come to feel more real than the other, disrupting the delicate balance of both/and. I adopt this Relational stance in making sense of the impact of the disabled sibling on the survivor sibling by cataloguing the three relational possibilities that emerged from the interviews themselves. It will become apparent that within each section, intra- and interpersonal elements intertwine as the data shift from experiencing the disabled sibling and the self as both fantasized objects and subjects in their own right.

I think our object world gets imposed on the subjects around us, whether or not we experience them as subjective objects or subjects in their own right, or back and forth in oscillating fashion (Benjamin, 1990; Ogden, 1989; Winnicott, 1971). I think most of us oscillate between subjective-object and subject-to-subject relating over the course of our lives many times; maturity in this sense is not a final destination, but a place to work at returning to. I think of defenses as if they are living tributes to one's most cherished inner objects and the relational patternings such objects allow for, always informed by an amalgam of inner experience and outer reality. Relationally speaking, we are only as "healthy" as our inner object world can allow. From this vantage point, we are always balancing the desire for new experience and growth alongside memorializing the familiarity of our inner objects through the enactment of certain self-states, which necessarily constrain in a felt-sense how far we are permitted to go. Every object has a series of self-states associated with it. The "self" of the survivor sibling shifts in and out from inner reality to externality, from a multitude of vantage points, some more referentially "me" and some "not-me." I believe that unconscious experience resides in both domains (intra-and inter-), and as Bromberg helps name, that we don't tell our unconscious fantasies, we *are* them (Bromberg, 2008).

Encountering experience requires regulatory functions and presence

What does all this talk of objects and subjects have to do with the developmental experience of survivor siblings? In order to encounter unexperienced-experience in real time (or at a later time), a containing reflective co-regulatory other is needed. This space rarely exists within the survivor sibling, prior to treatment. It must be built. And for reasons later discussed (see Chapter 4), the co-regulating containing reflective other is also in short supply in the original family experience. This mitigating factor, that is the absence of a protective other's mind for processing overwhelming direct experience and the unconscious fantasies it stirs in the self-system, has big consequences (Fonagy et al., 2002; Siegel, 2012). The other must be able to tolerate their own dissociative process in relation to the experience and find non-shaming ways to be with the survivor. Since caregivers are very often lost to their own survival, as well as managing the actual survival of their disabled child, survivor siblings encounter the harsh realities of this catastrophic loss/event and its lifelong attendant complications, often with a mentalizing other who shows significant deficits in the capacity to mentalize the experience of the survivor.

As I write this, I grow self-conscious and worry that disability activist organizations will rebuke me harshly for referring to the birth of a disabled child as catastrophic to the sibling/s. I do not mean to say that the identity of a disabled person is catastrophic, but the way a sibling experiences not having a peer who can engage in a reciprocal, mutual encounter – and one for whom this will never be a possibility in the full sense of reciprocity that accompanies equal capacities, even when age advances, coupled with a deficit in the capacity to process the event directly absent the mentalizing other – may be experienced as a catastrophic loss. The attendant medical crises are also a loss. I'd like to also remind readers that the severity of the disability, its chronicity, and its life limiting and threatening status are the conditions satisfied for participation in this study. What follows pertains to these circumstances, and not just any differences between siblings. So we are not talking about say a sibling with dyslexia and one without, or one with ADHD and one without, largely where treatment and services can mitigate the losses inherent in differential capacities.

I do not mean to imply that to be a survivor sibling of this kind is *only* a net loss. Some gains may be had through the experience of being a sibling to a disabled sibling too, but it's complicated. On the one hand, you have a sibling, but they do not operate interpersonally or intrapsychically the way other siblings seemingly can or do. This does not mean that there are no unique gains from having a disabled sibling, but I cannot wholeheartedly attend to the full picture if I have to censor myself out the gate by championing all the empathy and caretaking and intuitiveness that comes along with relating across difference, without addressing first the enormous sense of loss. Survivor siblings lose less-burdened caregivers and the chance of an abled-bodied and of sound, present minded sibling with whom to share the landscape of childhood. The thing we all lose is a capacity to be in time with ourselves and others. If we are lucky, we begin that way. The magic period of newbornness can startle everyone into the now. But then forces converge beyond our control to pull us to the future, or yank us back to the unresolved and/or unexperienced past, where life easily becomes a continual struggle to be in time, as it is. For the survivor sibling, external conditions preclude a chance of being in time, as is. There is no getting around acknowledging this, though many have tried by focusing on the gifts that the experience of otherness ushers in, including some of the interviewees (Solomon, 2012). This chapter though will offer a process related to the three thematic pathways of relational connection associated with the autobiographical experience of survivorship and siblings. The three relational realms that came into focus during the interviews include the following: (1) sensory overload and the felt-sense, (2) finding connection through caretaking, and (3) searching and relating through absence.

Sensory overload: connecting through the felt-sense

Thoughts, emotions, physical experiences, and senses are flooded with the arrival of a disabled sibling and this often continues chronically, if episodically, throughout development. The sensory overload is a place in which immediate resonance between each interviewee and myself is translated and often an area that gets underspecified and missed in other dyadic contexts. To me it feels most akin to veteran and war metaphors: Unless you have been there, it's very hard to convey an impression of the sights, sounds, smells, and images that fill the mind and body. The nature of physical abnormalities, cognitive and affective limitations, and the responses these episodes generate within the family and social milieu all carry a too-muchness quality, which ironically gets represented through dissociative silence later on. The intensity of the sensory stimuli obviously impacts the intersubjective environment and limits the kinds of connection available between family members. It's an area where survival is imminently present: The physical survival of the disabled sibling, and the emotional survival of the loved ones who provide the care and/or witness these scenes. Despite its obvious presence to those who were there, it very often gets missed and remains unimagined by those who did not go off, so to speak, to fight in the war. I can still recall vividly a sensorial experience I used to have on my then classically oriented analyst's couch of my legs being cut off below the knees. It came out of nowhere and it frightened me – but when I named it aloud, it was not connected to my survivor sibling experience of sensory overload or of my attempt to locate my brother in a body based way through somatic identification by either of us. For those who were born after their disabled sibling, the awareness of it being one specific moment is not there, as they entered into a world where this sensory overload already existed. For those born before the disabled sibling, a sensory imprint of time before and after – the hallmark of most PTSD conditions – is present. What do I mean by sensory overload? Let's turn to the data to hear the kinds of things survivor siblings took in, at very young ages.

Marisa, whose sister was born 3 years after her, had a severe genetic condition in which her parents had been told at the time that the life expectancy was no more than 20 years. The sensory overload on the cognitive/emotional level of knowing a sibling has a shortened life expectancy, and the weight of her parent's anticipatory grief, was always there. **Marisa** also endured her sibling's "excruciatingly painful bone crises," in which her sister's "extremely brittle and easily fractured bones would die from lack of adequate blood flow." **Marisa** elaborated how she would frequently awaken at night to the sound of her sister's "blood-curdling screams." She recalls the times between these episodes: "the normal times were never really normal." The soundtrack of unsoothable physical pain colored her early life.

Rose was born into a family with an intact older brother and a disabled older sister, her senior by two years. She attributed her parents' divorce when she was two to their enduring discrepancy and unresolvedness about whether to institutionalize her sister, who was placed in a home per the doctors' recommendations. As a teenager, **Rose** became curious why the family never visited this absent sister, and she went to see her. She recalls that it was "very upsetting, I felt very guilty, she was so disfigured, her chromosome had a break in it, she had some genetic condition." The hollowed out absence of her sister later took form and the image of her sister's physicality brought more sensory overload.

Susan was five years old when her mother returned home with her youngest disabled sister. Her sister's care "dominated family life." She shows me through visual recollections the extent to which the "dining room was converted into a therapy room." She often awoke to scenes of pain, and watched her parents "aspirate my sister's stomach, it was so gross, her stools were impacted. I just watched all this pain, agony and intrusive care."

Hannah is one of six siblings with a twin sibling with cerebral palsy. She experiences their twin connection through somatic mirroring at times. She tells me how her restless leg symptoms correspond to the multiple leg surgeries he sustained during his youth. She remembers his metal leg braces and how he'd frequently "lose control of his sphincter and get feces into the metal parts of the braces," alongside a recollection of her own inner monologue, which went "oh my god, get me out of here. . . . I'd dissociate a lot as his limbs would be all over the place, he couldn't control it."

Selena is one of five, whose younger brother by two years was born with cystic fibrosis. "We were told he was ill but not terminal," she says as she recalls her mom and brother spending a lot of time in the hospital and his oxygen mask. "I was a good sister, I'd connect the machine and clean up the vomit. We tried to help. He'd ask me, why do I take medicines and not get better?" Here the sensory overload includes not only the physicality but also holding the prescient knowledge of her brother's limited lifespan, alongside the vomit.

Rachel is the oldest of four siblings, the youngest of whom has cerebral palsy. She was seven when her sister was born and remembers being told that her sister suffered a trauma at birth. "So much of her disability is so loud and in your face and occupies so much of the space when she's present." She goes on to express how shameful it has felt to be frustrated by her reaction to the environment her sister creates.

Natalie, whose younger sister was disabled, recalls realizing more fully in latency the differences between them:

I think that somehow growing up with her made us perceive her as different, but normal. I generated a lot of pain when I got sick and did not know what the cause was; now I see that seeing my sister with so much pain and not being able to help her when she was [having] epileptic seizures for me was terrible. Sometimes I felt my stomach tearing and that there would be no way to close it again. And this feeling is what always comes back when I see someone suffer, of course it is not with the same intensity, but it has not disappeared. Having a sister with mental retardation marks you in a different way than other people . . . for me it was always more important to have a healthy body than worry about being beautiful, being able to do things that my sister could not do, as walking or talking to me is more important.

These represent glimpses into the kind of sensory experiences that were hard day after day in the lives of survivor siblings. The frequency though is not the point, because even those whose siblings resided in an institution were not spared knowledge of physical abnormalities and the attendant sensory and emotional overwhelm/overload on the individuals present and the caregiving system/environment. I think inhabiting the sensory overload is one of the more difficult places to attend. Dissociation from overwhelm happens precisely because the only way to down-regulate the experience is to evade it entirely. It actually was the impetus for this book, as I connected the experience of sleep training my son with memories of my own night terrors while witnessing my brother's seizures. My irritability and fear around my son's crying at night clued me in to what I had not let myself fully experience from these sensory overloads.

The impact of sensory overload is, of course, an increased need for self-regulatory skills, which are first found in the caregiving dyad between parents and children. But when parents' capacities are tapped out as a result of caring for the disabled sibling, and when the other sibling is impaired, it's highly probable that self-regulation for the survivor sibling is not well developed (Siegel, 2012). Any number of things can replace actual self-regulation, including of course the obvious psychoanalytic contenders of addiction, obsession, depression, attempts to consolidate the entirety of oneself in a false-self structure, and engaging in repetitive masochistic relations,[1] just to name a few (Khan, 1983; Winnicott, 1960). I do not claim that survivor siblings all gravitate toward any one particular thing, but sharing a deficit in self-regulation as children is a common thread, and it goes along with this sensory overload in their actual environment, plus whatever unconscious fantasies were stirred in response to this actual environment. There is no soothing for that which cannot be represented in the mind of the caregiver and then handed back in a containing way (Bion, 1962).

Caretaking as a pathway to connection

There are obstacles to mutual connection between survivor siblings and disabled siblings, but if you can't experience mutual reciprocity, you can still experience relatedness. It's the attachment literature that actually comes to mind, as survivor siblings are often endowed with the role of bigger or older one (no matter birth order) and connect to their sibling through forming an attachment based on caretaking. This is a very common portal available for connection for survivor siblings to their disabled siblings. While caretaking no doubt enhances compassion and creates a place for connection, it also invites both an imbalance and often further difficulties with self-regulation for survivor siblings. Particularly without the help provided by a reflective other during the tender developmental years, a survivor sibling is likely to introject the destructiveness of the disabled sibling's condition feeling it as something that resides within them and will identify their "nasty" feelings of envy, dread, shame, rage, grief, and helplessness as disabling confirmations of one's own lack of deservingness of life. What belongs to whom, and a densely populated inner space of projective processes, is likely to descend within the psyche of the survivor sibling, confusing the self-awareness underlying the motivations to care for one's siblings. The push and pull involved in holding oneself back to be with the sibling, versus the feared violence of moving forward developmentally, can readily dominate the inner experience. Take a listen now to the voices of survivor siblings looking for interpersonal connection and intrapsychic relief through the caregiving provided to their disabled siblings.

Marisa: "My sister's growth was greatly impacted by her condition, so when she was five, she appeared no more than two, and had beautiful striking physical features that lent a doll-like quality to her appearance."

Even with the chronic fractures, big back brace, and medical complications, **Marisa** felt herself to be the truly disabled one, as her sister's condition and beauty elicited the caretaking of everyone around them, including **Marisa** herself, who solidified her usefulness to her sister and parents by making her sister laugh. In talking with me she laments, "What about me? I became depressed and really conflicted about being successful. I had terribly low self-esteem and my body became very important to me, my appearance, but I couldn't see myself clearly. I feel completely damaged, destructive." Notice the tense change here as the past becomes present without pause. Later she tells me of a paper she gave at a conference years ago entitled, "To Kill Her or Cure Her," regarding her conflictual feelings of both protectiveness and rage toward her disabled sibling. These understandably ambivalent feelings left her feeling like a monster, like the one that was disabled for being filled with rage, helplessness, and love toward a sister whose life became the center of the family.

Susan has codified a professional identity around her abiding commitment to social justice, which began out of the legacy of caring for her sister in this way. The caretaking she provided included developing a "comfort using the non-verbal realm to forge relations." **Susan** tears up as she tells me how she'd relate to her sister through touch, tone, and presence, which she felt sometimes offset the guilt of "having more," and gave her a "gift of relating non-verbally at will." She is now unable to "turn off" the need to "give back."

Carolyn, one of multiple siblings, whose youngest sister by seven years was born with cerebral palsy, relays:

> Growing up I had a huge capacity for empathy, and caretaking. I accompanied my mom to the doctors and took on a lot of my sister's attachment needs, as we shared a bedroom too. My sister had no affect regulation and was anxious beyond control. Nights she couldn't settle down, it was my job to help her sleep. Infuriated, I felt helpless, but being her source of comfort and soothing also made me feel competent and important. Alone and scared, I felt I had to be an adult prematurely. Left me feeling burdened and depressed as a kid. I can still feel all of the chaos that ensued when she couldn't be soothed, she would scream and thrash and throw things.

Olina describes both siblings as impaired, but her brother had physical as well as emotional difficulties, whereas her sister was described as "almost normal" despite severe sensory issues. **Olina** honed in on her conflict around compulsory caretaking and the terror she encounters when she allows herself to feel negative feelings toward her siblings. She tells me she grows afraid of "what it will do to my body." She has reworked her early philosophy about there not being a limit to what you can give and seeks to identify her limits in an effort to challenge the early internalized other:

> *Reckoning with this loss and absence has shaped the course of my entire development. Ongoing mourning relationships not had with my siblings, and this heavy sadness that our aggression will never meet, I'm left wondering, who can meet me at the emotional level where I live?*

Darlene's younger sister by two years was born a "complete chromosomal disaster" and was given a life expectancy of five years. She fomented a caregiving relationship through their "tactile connection" and also took up the role of protector:

> *I remember being stared at when we'd be out as a family, and I'd stare right back at people, felt very protective of her. At times I could feel very angry at not having more of a sibling to relate to.*

Claire is one year older than her severely disabled brother, who relies on the family to survive. She attributes the dissolution of her parents' marriage when she was very young to their differential capacities in "accepting" her brother's diagnosis and the attendant lifetime of care it bestowed upon them. She remembers going to preschool and feeling her "neurotypicalness," while her brother remained non-verbal and learned sign language. Compassion, empathy and caretaking behaviors became prominent features of her interpersonal skills. But inside,

> *The guilt – it's hard to be related to my brother. Sometimes I forget I have a brother and this fills me with shame. It's like I'm an only-child, or someone with only the "downsides" of a sibling but not a lot of the upsides. Who do you talk about this with, because nobody understands such intense guilt, I feel like an awful person.*

Kira, from a multi sibling family whose youngest sibling by five years was severely and permanently disabled by medical error, explains that from a young age she learned how to administer medicines, oxygen masks, and to lift her up. Sometimes she'd stay up taking care of her sister overnight to give her parents a break. "We never talked about the ugly feelings, maybe we were all embarrassed of her." She describes experiencing night terrors herself as a child; she'd sleepwalk and her sister's nurse might find her in the bathroom crying. "I had lots of insecurity around abandonment and the fear that something like this could happen again, and was always looking out for the next intrusive medical event." But she tells me the caregiving gave her a tremendous capacity to mobilize in the face of crisis. She describes herself as the only remaining sibling in a stable marriage with children of her own. She continues to both need and desire a high-pressure environment for work as her "fascination with terrible things," and she attributes this to the thought, "I realize how badly life can go, and want to be on the helping side of it."

The caretaking experience is multifaceted, as you've just read. While it's my belief that it does not work so well at helping to differentiate psychically from the disabled sibling or the family, it does generate an interpersonal context of connection between siblings across the disability spectrum. There is something enchanting about having a special kind of connection, reaching soul to soul across difference, and so within the caretaking experience there are some gifts. A disabled sibling generally lives in the present, which a Buddhist psychological approach identifies as an enlightened capacity. If your life expectancy is shortened and/or if you lack language, ego-driven living makes much less sense, and a kind of meditative recognition that all any of us really have is the moment we are in pervades. These kinds of lessons can be imparted through contact between a survivor sibling and a severely disabled one. **Darlene** described getting into bed with her disabled sister during our interview, not knowing I had done the same thing with my brother, and she said, "There was something soothing and special about our quiet connection, of being with her that stripped the intensity away." **Susan** similarly talked very movingly about the ease with which she can relate to the nonverbal domain, through touch, facial expressiveness, and proximity; all the nonverbal cues she can give to convey her presence and register the presence of the other. Having a disabled sibling necessarily teaches you how to reach across certain divides for which ego and minds are not especially good vehicles. It makes you practice mindfulness well before you even know what mindfulness is! But it also, for me anyway, would highlight our difference: My brother's natural condition of being all-now, all this moment, and my difficulty being present in the moment would often translate into more loss. I was really struck by the interviewees who could meet their sibling in the now and be there with them long enough to take it in. Undoubtedly, the capacity to hold and work with silence and the nonverbal necessarily has its advantages in being a psychoanalyst.

Relating through absence

The other pathway available, both intrapsychically and interpersonally, for connection among survivor siblings to their disabled sibling may be found through absence. The longing for a sibling connection when there is a disabled sibling present, or when the sibling is actually absent via institutionalization (or later as a result of premature death), can be met by intrapsychically and interpersonally pursuing a relationship to the absence. Forging a long-term relationship to absence can take many forms, manifesting in actual searches for information that is withheld or not openly discussed in the family, through visits to the institution in which the sibling resides, from depressive structures which intrapsychically reserve a place for the lost sibling in effigy, and so on. Some survivor siblings relate fervently to the absence of their disabled sibling (again, whether literally or figuratively) instead of attending to the physicality of the sibling that is there. This relationship to absence and longing stands in for the relationship to the sibling. The quest to figure out what happened, while not being detected by caregivers, can take on a life of it's own.

Harold, whose younger brother with severe intellectual disabilities died when Harold was a teenager, described his entire childhood colored by his experience of being an "amateur sleuth detective." No words or explanations were given to him regarding his brother's condition, so he made it his mission to "connect the dots and discovered through snooping" evidence that his parents had considered a malpractice suit against the obstetrician for arriving late to his brother's delivery. **Harold** used his detective mission to deal with what continues to feel to him like a "ghost like absence" as his brother lived home with them for a short time, before he was suddenly and unceremoniously institutionalized. He tells me how betrayed he felt by his parents, who asked him how he'd feel about his brother "going away to school"; when he answered affirmatively without fully understanding the implications, he came home himself one day to find all of his brother's belongings, and his brother, gone. He was left feeling that he had sealed his brother's fate. His brother's health gradually deteriorated while institutionalized, and he ultimately died of pneumonia. **Harold** first sought him out emotionally by trying to find out what was wrong with him, through volunteering and connecting with the two other families in the housing development that had disabled children. He tells me:

> *Sometimes in the company of other families with similar circumstances, that became more informative to me than any exchange I had with my parents. My mother volunteered doing fundraising for. . . [a local non-profit] . . . and I would sometimes go to the buildings to collect the contribution envelopes.*

Ultimately, Harold was only able to form an attachment to the absence of his brother, on account of institutionalization followed by his untimely death. Working out the mystery of what had happened, and why, and what might happen next, became **Harold's** main way to relate to his disabled brother.

Selena, whose youngest disabled sibling ultimately died from cystic fibrosis when they were kids, tears up as she remembers being a child watching the eclipse with her family and seeing her disabled brother, the only one not wearing any sunglasses. Her parents knew his death was imminent, though she and her remaining siblings did not. Her parents kept them absent at the time of his death. Being absent from his death as well as any preparation that it was coming sent her on a psychic quest to identify and locate his experience. By the time she reached graduate school for psychology, she organized her thesis around the following theme: "What do children who are terminally ill think and feel?" Guilt, anger, low self-esteem, jealousy, difficulty using her own aggression, and trying to locate her lost sibling through her academic interests, are the ways in which she sustained her connection and attachment to her disabled sibling.

Debra was the fourth born to a middle-class family on the East Coast. She was initially very careful about participating in this study, imagining that she may not fit my profile for subject because her sister had been institutionalized before she was born. Her sister, who was three and a half years older than her, had been "born by planned C-section and was blind at birth followed by unsteady gains in normal infant development, which ultimately stopped altogether and reversed course at 16 months." Her parents sought the counsel of a neurologist who advised them to "institutionalize her and pretend she never existed." They did not listen to this first doctor, but eventually consulted another who also pointed toward institutionalization. "When I was born, my sister was not in the house. I'd notice when people asked my parents, 'How many kids do you have?' and they'd answer three." She tells me later when she was asked how many siblings she had that she was conflicted how to answer. Between ages 0 and 5, she visited her sister in the institution and recalls feeling "powerfully reassured by seeing her exist," but the visits dropped off, as she noticed her mom was unable to bring her sister pleasure anymore. She had no way of discussing this and saw the different ways institutionalizing her sister had wrecked both of her parents. So she struggled intensely but privately with her own fears of being discarded and getting sent away. As a child, she describes being super anxious without being able to tether this state to any understanding of her sister's absence. "I didn't realize how guilty I felt for possessing my intelligence as a survival tool, developed obsessionality and anxiety, and went from being very achieving to passive in adulthood, as I tried to reconcile this guilt."

None of these strategies of relating are consciously chosen, of course. They are the outcome of whatever the internal object world and the external circumstances allow. They are compromises, where contact with the other can be found, but often with very limited understanding of how identifying with caretaking or absence impacts internal self-development and the self-system in real time. These compromised formations are the space in which the relationship with one's sibling unfolds. Themes of ordinary competition and rivalry between siblings do not fit, unless one has a perverse view that zeros in on competing for parental attention in morbid contexts. Even here, an understanding that what generates parental attention is not based on who one is or is not, but instead on medical necessity, predominates the relational field and changes the meaning of what is typically thought of with sibling rivalry. No one is an actual winner here. Instead compulsive caretaking, attempting to connect through absorption in the now, and/or fantasies of reciprocity abound, as does a propensity to relate to absence. These options all foster a reliance on dissociative process as they leave out dimensions of the experience that are too hard to hold and bear within one's consciousness. Compulsive caretaking reduces the subjectivity of the survivor sibling to a function and values the self for doing rather than being. Connecting in the now (in the ways described here) denies what was lost in the past and minimizes the actual differences between siblings, to a point that may foreclose a capacity to mourn for what is/was lost. And giving in to fantasies of a kind of reciprocity that is not possible may widen the gap between the real and the imagined, unsettling the dialectical tension between fantasy and reality. And of course, relating to absence creates what Freud (1917) termed a melancholic structure, where a survivor's identity develops around the crater of what was lost. The silent explosion continues to affect the course of development for everyone, as these unmet longings and losses go unarticulated and are re-routed through the interpersonal strategies available to survivor siblings for contact.

Conclusion

Survivor siblings suffer an overload of difficult-to-integrate experience and a deficit of the kind of reciprocalness that transmutes traumatic experience into shared hardship. While the silver lining may be an early course in practicing presence in the now, these gains are only made possible in the context of what is lost. Necessarily, this results in survivor siblings' interior feelings of deficit, confusion, loss, anger, and unresolved grief/mourning. Everyone has what they experience as "damaged" parts of the self, and these parts are the ones most in need of containment and metabolization (Bion, 1959, 1962). But the survivor sibling is not likely to be able to access this kind of care during the primary years fostering a reliance on a dissociative structure to cope with living. This structure filters inhabited experience from the uninhabitable, further reifying the presence of unexperienced-experience. Let's turn to the attachment system, to gain a further understanding of why this is so.

Note

1 Masochism is a useful way to fool oneself into thinking you are practicing self-regulation skills by essentially saying, *hey, I'll self-regulate by controlling my environment.* All the one-person literature on masochism seems to speculate how gratifying it is to an impoverished ego to be humiliated and exploited, and many contemporary analysts no longer use the term given it's pejorative history from an objectivist standpoint. But a Relational take on masochism offers us the opportunity to realize a self that has no resonating other, cannot in fact, surrender, but can only submit to the dissociative structure in which it is reinforced (Ghent, 1990; Howell, 2013, etc.).

References

Benjamin, J. (1990). Recognition and destruction: An outline of intersubjectivity. In S. A. Mitchell & L. Aron (Eds.), *Relational psychoanalysis* (pp. 32–60). The Analytic Press.

Bion, W. R. (1959). Attacks on linking. *Psychoanalytic Quarterly, 82*(2), 285–300.

Bion, W. R. (1962). *Learning from experience.* Rowman & Littlefield Publishers, Inc.

Bonovitz, C. (2010). The interpersonalization of fantasy: The linking de-linking of fantasy and reality. *Psychoanalytic Dialogues, 20,* 627–641.

Bromberg, P. M. (2008). "Grown-up" words: An interpersonal/relational perspective on unconscious fantasy. *Psychoanalytic Inquiry, 28,* 131–150.

Chefetz, R. (2015). *Intensive psychotherapy for persistent dissociative processes: The fear of feeling real*. W. W. Norton Company.

Fonagy, P., Gergely, G., Jurist, E., & Target, M. (2002). *Affect regulation, mentalization and the development of the self*. Other Press.

Freud, S. (1917). Mourning and melancholia. In *The standard edition of the complete psychological works of Sigmund Freud, volume XIV (1914–1916): On the history of the psycho-analytic movement: Papers on metapsychology and other works* (pp. 237–258). London and Hogarth Press.

Ghent, E. (1990). Masochism, submission, surrender: Masochism as a perversion of surrender. *Contemporary Psychoanalysis, 26*, 108–136.

Howell, E. F. (2013). Masochism: A bridge to the other side of abuse (Revised). *Attachment: New Directions in Psychotherapy and Relational Psychoanalysis, 7*(3), 231–242.

Khan, M. (1983). *Hidden selves: Between theory & practice in psychoanalysis*. Karnac.

Kuchuck, S., & Sopher, R. (2017). Relational psychoanalysis out of context: Response to Jon Mills. *Psychoanalytic Perspectives, 14*(3), 364–376.

Ogden, P. (1989). *The primitive edge of experience*. Rowman & Littlefield Publishers, Inc.

Siegel, D. J. (2012). *The developing mind: How relationships and the brain interact to shape who we are* (2nd ed.). Guilford Press.

Solomon, A. (2012). *Far from the tree: Parents, children & the search for identity*. Scribner Simon & Schuster.

Winnicott, D. W. (1960). Ego distortion in terms of true and false self. In *The maturational process and the facilitating environment: Studies in the theory of emotional development* (pp. 140–152). Karnac.

Winnicott, D. W. (1971). The use of an object and relating through identification. In *Playing & reality* (pp. 115–127). Routledge.

Chapter 4

Reversals in caregiving

One rainy weekday morning as I am writing this book, my two-year-old son and I board the bus and watch a developmentally disabled wheelchair-bound boy of about three and his mother and father enter after us. My son grows quiet, noticeably taking in the scene before resuming his typical stream of consciousness outpour that is his usual toddler-speak. I immediately grow self-conscious as I feel the father's gaze rest on us for just a second, and as I see him next try desperately to straighten his son's face forward, while the boy continually arches his head sideways in an uneasy strain. I watch what I think of as a too-firm hand smooth and matte down the boy's hair to conceal the effort at manipulating the musculature of his child, under the cover of a caring gesture. The too-much pressure revealing what I imagine to be this father's underlying desperation that he hopes a quick pat conceals, while the child keeps straining his torso and face left. His mother looks forlorn. There in body only, her depressive absence filling me with shame for having the talkative, able-bodied child on my own lap. My mind races with recollections of my own parents enlisting my help in "calming" my brother down because the facial/spinal twisting usually came just before the onset of a seizure. I wonder whether our bus companions fear the same fate for their son, or if it's more a desire to "appear normal," as in, "at ease," that motivates this particular paternal intervention.

Memory transports me to the way back of the navy blue velour covered seat in the wheelchair-accessible van of my childhood. My dad driving the van, my mother in the passenger seat beside him, from my young self's perspective, leaving me about the distance of one subway car behind them both. I'd obey the request to "go calm your brother down" when given from the front seat as I'd unbuckle my own seat belt, grounding my toes into the carpet beneath my feet as I tried steadying myself against the movement of a car in motion, walking towards my brother whose wheelchair was suspended by all four points of the seat belt midway between me and my parents. I'd grab one of his closed-fisted hands, and with the other hand straighten his torso while I said something soothing. Often I'd feel a sense of frustration that my words did not work to alter his musculature or tension and resort to trying to make his face forward too, with force just like I imagine of this father on the bus. Occasionally this was enough to calm him – or perhaps the seizure was not going to happen anyway – but it felt like I had helped. A real un-reality remains about whether our loving, albeit desperate, interventions staved off further medical distress or if it was just a case of correlation.

Present tense, my mind returns to the too eager father now stroking his son's hair and head, trying to make this experience just fit, just face forward, just keep going, while the mother appears drowning at sea, having gone Edna Pontellier on the whole thing. I feel a sense of gratitude well up in me that my mom evaded that depression, that particular kind of melancholic mourning, where I would no doubt have felt her absence even more than I already did. Although her approach brought a whole host of other complications for me, I had her voice and her engagement, whereas this mother seems lost entirely to her grief. And then I feel bad – who am I to judge these parents? Maybe being openly depressed like that is more internally honest than dissociating and minimizing the impact of the disability on both the child and the whole family's life, turning tragedy into a fun game of a "definitely surmountable obstacle" with no end in sight, as my mother had seemingly done? After all, it looks like it has only been three years since she became a mother to this child. How long should a parent mourn? A younger part of myself then worries that their real/imagined envy of my "neurotypical son" is dangerous to me and will somehow manifest in some very ill fortune coming our way, obsessive thinking being the salve for fear in these moments. A quick detour down berating myself for being so self-centered to think I even register in their minds follows. And shortly behind that is the guilt, as I wonder briefly, how did I get a different experience of parenting than my own parents had? If I came from them, how did I get so far away? I'm lost in these thoughts and feelings as I come to realize I'm also not imagining other riders on the bus having a similar internal experience. I do not imagine I have other company here, and I want my facial expression to convey some understanding, some kinship with and to these parents before me – but all I have is a gregarious toddler in an especially good mood on my lap. There's no way they can see me seeing them from inside something. As we get off the bus, I'm troubled by this gulf between those who live this experience and those who do not.

Multiplicity, attachment, and attunement: a complex scene

Writing this chapter is very difficult. Openly discussing the feelings toward one's parents as a survivor sibling is hard – not just for me, but for all those I interviewed. The ability to talk about emotional and physical deprivations encountered as survivor siblings within the vertical axis goes along with fear of harming parents and the shame surrounding self-examination as it redirects attention away from the ones who really need it. After all, it is the disabled sibling and the parents who are the main characters in the literature and public imagination here, and this is reinforced and reinscribed culturally in how issues of disability are represented. Literature is there for parents adjusting to "Holland" (Kingsley, 1987) and for the disabled themselves, who rightfully so have a range of advocates giving voice to their perspective and experience (Batshaw et al., 2007; Solomon, 2012; Vargas & Prelock, 2004). The disabled also increasingly and thankfully have characters, real and imagined, representing their plight in television shows, nonprofits, and storylines (TheArc.org, Perspectivescorporation. com, etc.). But who speaks of the survivor siblings' experience[1]?

More than once I end up telling interviewees that I would not have been able to write this book were my mother still alive. Nevermind write it, I might not have been able to think it. There is so much fear associated with elaborating on an experience that could easily be read as "finger pointing" or blaming maternal/paternal deprivations, an anti-feminist/humanist agenda if ever there was one. Even if I try to do justice to all the subjective spaces within families such as ours, and look at this complex situation from many lenses, the empathy for a parent to a severely disabled child seems to eat up most of the room that might have otherwise been left over for wrestling with the impact of caregivers' vulnerabilities on the survivor siblings themselves. On more than one occasion, an interviewee would venture forth in sharing a particular detail that revealed/exposed the parent's vulnerability and its impact on the teller, and it followed quickly with a request that I not include *that content* in the book. Implicitly and explicitly protecting parents from further (real and imagined) harm becomes a big part of a survivor sibling's legacy.

How do we let ourselves think about and experience an area rife with internal conflict that is still active (for me, even in death!)? It helps me to focus on the questions such deprivations invite rather than the limitations that generate them. So for example, maybe there were no other ways of going through the experience of birthing and raising a disabled child than the dissociative structure adopted by most caregivers, but this structure became an inheritance for the survivor sibling.

Stern calls this kind of survivorship "airless world syndrome" to evoke the "identificatory bondage to the internalized negating" parent adopted by survivors, "which is disabling to the senses of self and personal agency and impairs the capacities to think, feel in an integrated way, separate and grieve" (Stern, 2019, p. 435). But how does this legacy of caretaking for the parents' psyches, whether or not it was asked for (consciously or unconsciously), affect survivor siblings' sense of self as they grow? I wonder a lot about this and argue with my mother on the Other Side. I ask, *What does she feel about my writing this book*? I worry too, of my father reading the book and feeling either misunderstood or blindsided. I read into everyone's reaction when they learn about my writing this and interpret too long a silence in response to my description of the topic, as an indication to censor myself. But why? As noted in the previous chapter, survivor siblings tend to be overly identified with the caregiving role and assume and partake in relating to the disabled sibling and the parent/s alike, oftentimes more like a parent than a sibling/child. Maybe this leakage or ill-defined inner boundary lends itself to a too-easy identification with the parents' experiences themselves so that speaking to the black holes in the attachment experience can feel like "attacking" the parents, which in turn becomes an "attack" on the self? There is also the obvious exposure to the conscious and unconscious content regarding the parent's feelings of responsibility, protectiveness, culpability, guilt, and loss regarding the disabled child, which get absorbed very easily in the unconscious psyche of the survivor sibling. As we know, projective processes go both ways from child to parent and parent to child all throughout childhood (and beyond). This dizzyingly multidirectional field is difficult to make sense of clinically and theoretically.

Frank Putnam (2016) developed a Behavioral States Model to capture the complexity of the multiplicity within self-experience that is present for everyone. In this model, how we are in any given moment replaces who we are. Flexibility, capacity to own contradiction, and awareness of the variability within state-dependent learning replace personality constancy.

In other words, we are all state-dependent creatures and the adaptability of the inter-systemic self-system we develop around our identities is contingent on the caregiving resonance experienced over the course of development. For survivor siblings, this systematic flexibility is impaired by the selective attention given to specific self-states by caregivers and the negation of others. This negation on the part of a caregiver need not be conscious to still be impactful. Structural dissociation of the personality is initially generated by trauma but becomes self-reinforcing through the maintenance of disorganized attachment systems that encourage avoidance and segmentation of not-me states (Chefetz, 2015; Van der Hart et al., 2006). Instead of reveling in the creative multiplicity of self (experience), many survivor siblings develop deep fissures between tolerable/permissible ways of being and intolerable not-permissible ways of being oneself that are, at least initially, determined by the allowances of the caregiving field in which the self is developed.

In this chapter, I will illuminate some of the self-state configurations of survivor siblings in relation to their caregivers as revealed by the narrative data. My focus will be on those self-states in particular that either get left out of the caregiver's field of vision or fail to be mediated by it, but nonetheless remain integral to a survivor sibling's sense of self.

Micro-traumatic attachments and self-development

Crastonopol's (2015) concept of micro-traumatic experiences, which she defines as repetitive subtly injurious patterns of engagement is apt in capturing the lopsided experience between survivor siblings and their parents. One such patterning she defines as "uneasy intimacy," in which:

> Role boundaries are more like regions than sharp edges, and within such a region, there is much room for the push and pull of confidence-sharing, attitude-influencing, {and} over-identification with another's internal objects . . . overtime this culminates in a kind of emotional exploitation, where there is a clear imbalance in whose inner world is getting protected and attended to at the expense of the other's "thriving."
>
> (p. 89)

Notice here that the configuration lends itself to an imbalance, in that the promotion, well-being, and maintenance of one person's inner world gets prominence so that the dyadic encounter is built up around this unspoken goal. The traumatic fallout from this dynamic may at first be barely detectable, but over time, this imbalance promotes the subtle erosion of what may have otherwise been a deepening subjectivity within the survivor sibling. Winnicott, too, speaks of those children who grow around such parental impingements, unaware initially that it costs them an encounter with their truest-self (Winnicott, 1965). The lopsided relationship is evidenced behaviorally in the ways survivor siblings prioritize emotional caretaking of their parents in whatever form that particular family needs, at the risk of inhabiting their own inter-systemic self-system with caregivers. Survivor siblings also often join parents in the caretaking of the sibling, or if the sibling is institutionalized, take up the need to bury questions and doubts about the decision to institutionalize, to protect parents from facing the imagined pain they'd encounter by their own inquisitiveness. Survivor siblings learn to split off[2] their natural curiosity and wonderings in order to deliver relief to the family system that is often wrought with more than anyone imagined having to handle affectively, physically, and cognitively. The dissociative maze surrounds and engulfs the entire family system. When you have independent mobility, when you have language, it can come to feel like navel gazing to a survivor sibling to peak inside at what remains unfed in them. Ergo what doesn't get reflected cannot be experienced, and so the pool of unexperienced-experience grows. Howell (2016) writes:

> In dissociative problems in living, the mutuality of relationships, between people as well as within the organization of the self, has largely collapsed or is missing. The person can only rely on the self and this creates a relatively closed system of the personality to compensate for the missing mutuality.
>
> (p. 33)

With this framework in mind, it becomes possible to say something about the extent to which survivor siblings both consciously and unconsciously become tied to helping parents maintain the defenses generated by this life experience, rather than encounter the mourning process, which risks disrupting them. Everyone's psychic survival comes to depend on this unconscious contract. Both parents and kids come to feel they are prospectively harmed by efforts, conscious or otherwise, that rob their parents of the attitudes, beliefs, behaviors, and ways of being, which were adopted to live the legacy of parenting a permanently and severely disabled child.

One such adaptation commonly grasped among parents is the need to view the nondisabled child(ren) through an idealized lens. The idealization itself is not as damaging as the inability to see or resonate with the (damaged) parts of the survivor sibling. Others have discussed the pressure that comes along with being idealized, but I want to emphasis the damage that occurs when one's negative *not-me* states are not met with containment. Siegel (2012) puts forth a neuroscientific and evolutionary perspective that shows how making sense of other minds gives us a sense of self that is durable, coherent, and ongoing and that this sense-making begins within the parent–child matrix. A hallmark of secure attachment is an ongoing capacity to integrate intra- and interpersonal experience within the self, through the utilization of the parent's resonance with their child's states of mind. But for the survivor sibling, whose parents tend to exaggerate their capacities and deny, minimize, or ignore their limitations, there is no resonance for the *negative parts of self* to be integrated. From a multiple self-state perspective, parent's psychic survival strategies can inadvertently reinforce survivor sibling's need to dissociate or bury not-me "negative" states outside self/other awareness on the basis of their own attachment needs.

A lopsided attachment system comes into play where security between survivor siblings is found in the expression of permissible self-states, while the negative ones that threaten parental security remain untouched and unmediated. If, as Seigel states, "co-construction, contingent, collaborative communication reflecting on the mental states that contribute to a shared subjective experience is central to secure attachment" (p. 333), what happens to survivor siblings, whose "bad" (as in non-permissible) self-states fail to enter the co-constructed space with a parent? Hopenwasser (2018) defines attunement as "an embodied rhythmic encounter that facilitates the management of unbearable pain in a shared healing experience" (p. 48). With no relational context or a severely limited one to manage those parts of the survivor sibling that hold pain, fear, anger, and loss, this lack of resonance with a caregiver puts survivor siblings at greater risk for dissociative disorders (Chefetz, 2015; Howell, 2016; Schore, 2009; Siegel, 2012).

If we return to a loosely integrative multiplicity as the cornerstone of subjective experience and note the greater the presence of trauma, the more self-states may be generated and the more fragmented or nonreflective these self-states are from one another, we can imagine that various identifications of survivor siblings carry different attachment styles to their parents (Bromberg, 1996, 1998). Attachment scholars code attachment as a discrete variable of coherence across self-states, and in such a conceptualization, disorganized, and insecure attachments would permeate the whole system (Lyons-Ruth et al., 2006). Of course, however, for the purposes of understanding the subjective experience of survivor siblings, I wonder if some tentative or intermittently imagined secure attachment might exist alongside the disorganized and insecure care-taking? And if so, to what effect? Siegel writes:

> Not all individuals are able to find emotional well-being in integrating multiple self-states into a coherent experience of the self. From early in development, the resolution of multiple models of attachment may be one of the determinants of later developmental outcome. Particular forms of self-states may have been constructed in relationship to different caregivers, resulting in potentially conflicting conditions. The capacity for such internal integration may be intimately related to interpersonal experience derived initially from attachment relationships.
>
> (p. 310)

I'll leave it to the reader to wonder whether my suggesting a space of secure connection between survivor siblings and their parents, alongside deeply insecure and onerous ones, is just further evidence of a survivor sibling's need to resurrect something good from the parents and to insulate them from imagined harm, itself a by-product of loyalty to a dissociative process. Maybe this is as good as it gets in a dissociative family system. But I do hear evidence of admiration, connection, and love alongside deeply held insecure/disorganized ties in the narratives that follow. There are moments in my own experience and in the interview subjects' memories of parents that resonate and create a tentative connectedness around the experience of being together, if not outright around survivorship. I'd also like us to consider the implications for the multiple transferences that might arise in the treatment of a survivor sibling vis-à-vis the analyst given this picture, some more "secure" than others. If Bromberg (and others) emphasize the primacy of multiple self-states in all of us, you could call on Fairbairn's (1963) conceptualizations of the varying affective object relations housed *within* one self toward the same actual other as a model for the multiple kinds of attachment styles that I am describing. Something exciting, something enlivening, something frightening, something rejecting, and so on separated by these dissociative barriers between them.

What is undisputed in the literature is the mutative impact of reflectivity in the dyad. It is the cornerstone of mental health and resiliency in self-development. Siegel (2012) writes: "reflective dialogue is centrally related to integrative capacities, and parents who can't do this around certain areas impoverish the kids capacity to feel coherent as a self" (p. 333). This is through no intentional fault of the parent's own, but instead a result of their own wound/s and dissociative ways of managing them. As the intergenerational perspective reveals, absence begets absence. Boss (1999) writes:

> If families are to care for their chronically ill loved ones when there are few answers, they need help sorting through the emotions that accompany caregiving work in the context of ambiguity. They need to know what effects unresolved grief has on family members.
>
> (p. 50)

Boss ultimately endorses dialectical thinking – and I'd elaborate to say *experiencing* – as the goal for treatment of losses that remain unclear and indeterminate among families. A lopsided attachment collapses the dialectical space necessary for processing. Ongoing frozen grief lends itself to dissociative processes in families that shut down dialectical thinking/experiencing, compromising integrative features in the family system as a whole, and within each person individually.

Often the side of a survivor sibling's experience that lacks mental representation within the caregiving system is the "negative" not-me states, which vary by person and family. It is a privilege to hear the interviewees grapple with the consequences encountered in the complex attachment system developed with their parents. Again, each case itself is unique, but for purposes of illustration, I have organized the contents into the following thematic expressions: (1) Overidentification with parents and one-sided mentalization, (2) Fears of separation, (3) Failed efforts at getting one's bad self-states contained in the mind of a caregiver, and (4) Impact of the absence of parental mentalization on inter-systemic self-development.

Overidentification with parents and one-sided mentalization

The uneasy intimacy fostered by the closeness described by Crastonopol (2015) results in a confusion of boundaries between survivor siblings and their parents. Another way of putting this is that the child becomes accustomed to (speaking/living) the parents' language rather than the other way around (Ferenczi, 1949). Listen to how Ferenczi (1949) describes what his patients with trauma histories experience in the transference while in treatment:

> Gradually, then, I came to the conclusion that the patients have an exceedingly refined sensitivity for the wishes, tendencies, whims, sympathies and antipathies of their analyst, even if the analyst is completely unaware of this sensitivity. Instead of contradicting the analyst or accusing him of errors and blindness, the patients identify themselves with him; only in rare moments of an hysteroid excitement . . . can they pluck up enough courage to make a protest; normally they do not allow themselves to criticize us, such a criticism does not even become conscious in them unless we give them special permission or even encouragement to be so bold.
>
> (p. 225)

In this unconscious adaption to the one who is bigger, parts of the self go unfed. The absence of a more mediated self-awareness is filled in with a *heightened* awareness of the parent's actual or imagined state of mind. This achieves three things: 1) It rids survivor siblings of having to face and feel the parts of self-experience for which there is no empathic other, 2) it allows them an illusion of control in tracking and knowing all about their parent's state of mind, and 3) it provides them with information they can use to anchor the attachment, by delivering what the uneasy alliance may call for from them relationally speaking. Let's turn to some examples to demonstrate the tenacity of identification with the parent's states of mind.

Marisa knows her mother's story as though she were her biographer. She tells me how her mom originally wanted five children, but after her younger disabled sister was born, she had no more kids. She watched the mom she knew who used to dress in "*beautiful clothes from Paris, and sing and dance*" begin to wear "*only black and blue dresses*." The change signaled something big to her. She intuited her mom felt she no longer had a right to "*dress up.*"

Because it was a fragile bone condition my sister had to be watched like a hawk, which meant my mother could never take her eyes off of her. I developed a lot of ambivalent feelings toward my mother. I couldn't

be alone. My mom was a good psychologist, she'd help me under-
stand why my sensitive, artist father was angry. He'd come home and
kick the dog and she would explain to me, "there's something called
projection, he gets angry instead of crying (about your sister)." I was
mostly so nice, I had to be so nice. . .

Here we imagine how **Marisa's** mom used her mind to protect herself
from being overwhelmed by the condition of her disabled child and dys-
regulated husband, as she implicitly coaches **Marisa** to do the same. She
enlists **Marisa** in taking a similar stance, filling her with knowledge about
psychological phenomena that acted as a salve to her as an adult but would
not have the same effect on a kid. This reveals the internal confusion of
speaking between mother and daughter and begs the question, who is
actually helped by "having information" about psychological defenses?
Having information is rarely an adequate substitute for having a mediated
experience with a caregiver. **Marisa** holds on to the attachment through
careful record keeping of her mother's story, close tracking of changes in
her state, behavior, and appearance, and in effect, seems as observant of
her mother as her mother is of her sister.

Susan has been a historian of her parents' lives, as she tells me about
a ritual that she codified in adulthood of interviewing her parents and
recording these sessions. She asks them questions all about their life experiences but has omitted any exploration of her disabled sister, who is now
deceased. She tells me, it's "*one topic that is still very off limits.*" When
I ask her how she knows this is so, she shares that even as a child: "*My
parents did not want to talk about it, and I could not tolerate their silence.
But I haven't invaded it either.*" Given her direct presence regarding other
emotionally charged topics that require her to challenge them a bit, it is
striking that she preserves and maintains the dissociative silo around an
experience that no doubt shaped all of them very much. In talking with
her, I can feel how she lands on a "don't ask, don't tell" policy regarding
her sister for her parents' benefit. And as she elaborates on her own grief
journey in adulthood related to this sister, I note how this happens outside
the space of parental resonance even long after her sister passed away.

Carolyn gives an account of two different parental responses and seems
to track both of them in her field of vision and narrative. She describes
a preoccupied father, whose story surrounding her sister's disability is
porous and changes as he ages, but in each iteration highlights a heightened sense of responsibility on his part, whereas her mother is "*harder to*

interpret, emotionally much more detached. I think she was depressed. She doesn't really talk about it. She was all devotion, duty and dedication to her care." She goes on to tell me how much she fears her parents' death, as she will be the sibling most likely to inherit the caretaking responsibilities for her disabled sibling. She reflexively enacted caretaking her sister and her parents as a child but is quite burdened by this. As soon as she reaches awareness of feeling burdened, it is met with the fantasy that she will be identified in this book by her family and found "*fault*" with for giving voice to their absence in her emotional world:

I felt like there wasn't an adult around. In recognizing how much my parents were unable to help my sister, I felt I had to be the adult, but then it didn't feel like adults were there to help me either. My parents relied on me to take care of her a lot, and later they relied on me to advise them about how to take care of her. It was a lot to manage.

Rose, whose parents separated shortly after her sister was institutionalized, described her mom's fragility as lifelong, and reenacted this for me, as she huddled into a quiet corner of her room with her door closed for our interview by Skype because, as I later learned, her mother and brother were visiting and in another part of her home at the time of our call. Her positioning for our call, taking shelter on the ground behind a closed door, enacted in form the feelings and experiences she related in words:

There was no discussion, my mom, she was not ok. My dad had set a tone, he did not want to know my sister was a person, and my mom obeyed, for her own reasons . . . I was extremely attuned to my mom, and how she was doing. As a girl it was like we were one person, I [was] very focused on her wellbeing, needing her to know that I was ok. She was never great at my not being ok. I'd go to her for support, but [would] quickly realize she needed me to support her. I'm still very tied up with her wellbeing, and hyper aware of my impact on other people.

Olina relays how her mom stayed home when her three kids were young, two of whom were disabled. While she always had information from her parents regarding both siblings' disability conditions, she never felt she had "*true permission*" to talk about her feelings directly with them. She intuited and has lived with a sense that she is the "*compensation prize*" to her parents leaving her with an "*un-realistic sense of timing*" and unwieldy relationship to her own needs for attention and attachment. *"The other deal"* she felt she made to keep things stable was that she could not know her anger. She tells me that is too active a phrase for how it came about at the time. Her parents being available in some sense was *"reasonable."* In piecing it together as we spoke, she identified that to be angry felt like an attack on her parents or her more vulnerable siblings, even though she had survived to be something they could never be, she was to be humbled by that, always. She felt she had to be *"emptied of aggression"* to take care of her parents' needs and embody perpetual gratitude for her *"neuro-typical"* self. Again the parental field of vision does not allow many degrees of affective freedom or expression.

Rachel, whose disabled sister was born when she was 7 years old, remembers first her mom's *"delay"* in coming home after the traumatic birth of her sister. She has to date, remained extensively close with her mother, talking daily, but notably, *"not about this"*:

> *My Mom went above and beyond to try to make my life normal, my friends growing up knew my sister, and I never felt embarrassed to have friends over, which is a testament to my mother, who also made time for me without my sister around.*

Listen to how she credits her mom for not being in touch with any discordant feelings **Rachel** had as a child about her sister's condition. It is a not so subtle representation of what this section highlights, that it is far more prevalent to identify with the parent's experience than having the internal space and freedom to discover one's own experience. Later **Rachel** elaborates how despite her mom's efforts to normalize home life, she knows she also felt her mom was absent and preoccupied. *"I did not know it then, but I think I experienced her absence through somatization, developing stomachaches and separation anxiety."* Overly identified with the parental state, **Rachel** tells me she thinks daily about what it must be like for her mom to have a dependent child in her seventies. *"Anxiety and depression remained throughout my life on and off, and I developed by necessity, a flexible personality. I'm easy-ish, roll with the punches but that's just on the outside."* She acknowledges some difficultly staying connected with what she actually feels, in order to *"roll with things how they are"* and situates herself inside her mother's experience of hardship, as one way to stay connected even as it costs her knowing more fully what she feels inside her own self-system.

Debra was the third born of four children with an older disabled sister, and she does not recall a time not knowing she had this sister, despite her sister having been institutionalized for the duration of **Debra's** life. **Debra** has early memories of visiting her sister at the institution with her parents and brother. "*My father would never talk about her so it was very obvious not to ask him. My mom would answer my questions, but did not initiate.*" She describes a "*rocky*" adolescence, as she tested her father's fragility and he responded by disclosing contents of his fantasies of defeat and revenge toward her sister's "*unfixable condition*" and the pain that accompanied it. "*My father seemed cold and angry and mom more furtive and ambivalent, they never understood what had actually gone wrong and they dealt with it in these different ways.*" Here, too, we learn of **Debra's** observations and making-sense of her parent's experience, exactly the kind of resonating Siegel (2012) describes only in the opposite direction than optimal for childhood. **Debra** tests her dad's loyalty to her and the family during adolescence but quickly learns more than she can bear to hold as a result. This leads to its own re-traumatization, as opposed to healing, and heightens her own sense of fear around being discarded and gotten rid of if she is "bad."

Natalie not only identified with the parent perspective but also has turned this identification into a professional achievement by publishing about the parent's experience of caregiving for medically complex children. She is a survivor sibling, but her professional attention is absorbed in remembering and imagining her mother's experience of this. She tells me her father was silent and did not say much about it, but she watched her mother devote herself to her sibling's care. Rather than feel her mother's absence, she attempted to find her through an undifferentiated identification with her:

> *I think it was also because after 13 years I helped my mother a lot to take care of her. For this reason, the bond I had with my sister, for me, was very special. I think I can even say that it was [my sister] who helped me the most to develop as a human being, as well as my parents, so I cannot say that being aware of [my sister's disability] has generated particular symptoms in me.*

If attunement means meeting someone in the experience they are having, uneasy intimacy means losing hold of one's own experience in place of experiencing the important bigger other/s. Of course, no parent asks their survivor sibling child to do this, and many (and most), I am sure, are not walking around hoping their children will heal their own inner wounds. And yet, these examples show to what lengths survivor siblings are holding their parents' psychic integration in mind and heart throughout development up through the present. It is easy to see and feel how their own affective experience gets sidelined or put off to the margins. In and of itself, that would not be a "bad" thing, but without a mentalizing other to transform the contents into something not toxic to the self, the reversal of attachment system here has big implications. The psychic errand of healing one's parents never actually works and it comes at way too high a price for healthy self-awareness and development. Not to mention that it supports rather than deconstructs a dissociative structure. Being a parent's biographer is no way to live a life.

Fears of separation

In addition to close observation of the parents, another way survivor siblings may express an insecure and disorganized attachment system is through anxiety. A very common experience among survivor siblings is to activate the attachment system through the experience of fear. A particular fear that is encapsulated in the content of unexperienced-experience is that of separation. Fears regarding separation may be signaling outside and inside the self-system – outside, to the parents for creating proximity, and inside to the self-system, as a way of bringing to consciousness those self-states that typically remain outside awareness. Again, returning to Winnicott, if the thing we fear has already happened (just existing outside our conscious recognition), one way we might conceive of separation anxiety is that the survivor sibling can better tolerate the absence of parts of their own experience when they are oriented with others and that being actually alone can stimulate an unwanted awareness of one's own dissociation. If the system of dissociative adaptation thrives on attention to the Other, the absence of the actual Other presents a challenge to the equilibrium of the dissociative structure. One may come to feel that they are left alone (again) with one's unwanted selves.

Marisa elaborates, "*Because it was a fragile bone condition my sister had to be watched like a hawk, which meant my mother could never take her eyes off of her. I developed a lot of ambivalent feelings toward my mother. And I couldn't be alone.*" She tells me that when she went away to college she was sexually assaulted early on, which among other things provided a rationale for her coming back home, but also met her need to be back home beside her mother.

Harold, with a disabled younger brother by two years, lived at home with his parents until marriage. So frightened he was of being banished as his brother had been during his elementary school years to an institution, he could not bear to leave the insecure security of his parents' literal home until marriage, among perhaps other concrete reasons.

Hannah relays that her mother survived her brother's cerebral palsy by "*converting powerlessness into agency, believing she'd been endorsed by God to raise a disabled child, and relishing in being 'needed'.*" When **Hannah** would tentatively inquire about the finite amount of maternal love and attention her mother responded with, "*I love the one who needs me most.*" **Hannah** managed her disorganized attachment by dissociating and more than any other interviewee explained how her body carried the experiential knowledge that was split off from her family's consciousness, perhaps also connected to her being a twin of her disabled sibling. "*Our whole family revolved around his care. Nobody ever said to me, it's fine to be normal, I don't love you any less.*" When she went away to college, she tentatively tried to raise her fears around separation to her mother, who she said "*made me feel small for bringing them up in the first place given that I was not the one living the disability.*"

Olina recalls:

> *Feeling shame around my needs and dealing with that shame by going to extremes, either not asking for help or playing helpless to access help. This made for rocky development in that I was pushed into things before I was ready, like skipping kindergarten and going into first grade, making up for the steps my other siblings couldn't take – so much guilt around being "okay" but also wanting to deliver that experience to my parents. Even though I feared separation.*

Kira, whose sister's disability occurred as a result of a severe adverse reaction to an accidentally administered vaccination at 18 months of life, describes her mother as appearing to have experienced the "death" of her sister at the time of this incident. **Kira** recalls as a child getting the courage up one day to say to her mom, "*You love* [disabled sibling] *more than us,*" and her mom replied, "*Oh, I hope you don't think that.*" But mom failed to take it as an opportunity to hear Kira's concern. **Kira** interrupts the story as she tells me to remark on her own dissociation of affect: "*I can't feel the* *tears but I know they are somewhere inside.*" The double injury of not having her experience validated by her mom, and being instructed to "*think*" (or not to think) one's feelings, as opposed to experiencing them, remained present tense. Throughout the interview, she struggles to embody the self-state of her asking for her mother's attentive presence as well as the self-state lamenting her absence.

Debra tells me the fear was ever present: "*I was a super anxious child without understanding the source of it. As I grew, I struggled with how well I was surviving, am I allowed to survive so well?*" Of the very few things her mother has directly said to her about her sister, she tells me how one day her mom began: "*I want to tell you why I was able to let go of your sister and be so free and easy*" and she stopped her, "*I can't hear that mom. My mom's unconscious guilt lives inside of me.*" But **Debra** had to provide her own protection, as her mom had not imagined this. "*There is such a loyalty in your parent's creation of what the story is, how do you say anything that's more essential to you without hurting the people you love?*"

Rachel recalls the 8-hour-a-day traumatic brain injury program her sister was enrolled in and how much time was spent in making sure she got care, while she also remarked how careful her mom was to protect her by making room for her to have a social life and strong academic life. Despite these notable efforts, **Rachel** described experiencing intense separation anxiety, which often took the form of "*stomachaches*" and fears around bathroom accessibility.

I can chime in here to say that I too suffered severe separation anxiety throughout most of my childhood/young adult years. I transferred it onto romantic relationships by the time I reached high school and college, but it was no less debilitating in that arena than the original home environment. It is a strange feeling to fear being apart from the very thing that is also contributing to your own dissociative process. Subjectively speaking, it is a kind of imprisonment for which there is no felt relief. One of the things that I believe binds this kind of fear is the unknown but felt necessity of needing to transmute the badness inside oneself through the attachment system. Of course as kids, no one is thinking of it this way, but there is this hope that a day will arise when the parents might be able to provide the psychic relief that is sought. Being apart from them, and later substitute attachment objects, can induce a fear of missing a moment when resonance might be found and also of contacting oneself without any distraction, which leads to the next category of attachment-related experiences often encountered among survivor siblings.

Failed efforts at getting bad-me/s seen

If Siegel gives us a biological understanding of the function of attachment on the developing self, Bion provides an intrapsychic view in his principals related to containment and metabolization, as shown by the projective process within the caregiving dyad. Part of the difficulty of gaining recognition and resonance of not-me self-state experiences is that often they do not (yet) exist in thought form during development (and beyond, depending on what follows). Bion (1962) writes:

> Beta-elements are stored but differ from alpha-elements in that they are not so much memories as undigested facts, whereas the alpha-elements have been digested by alpha-function and thus made available for thought.
>
> (p. 7)

Absent the transformation from beta to alpha, the experience of dissociated not-me states remain active within the survivor sibling without conscious and/or symbolized connection to the self or those outside the self. New traumatic events may elicit the undigested, unprocessed content, as the dam of beta elements erupts, often outside even the awareness of the one whose material it is that's spilling forth. I am thinking of this as I listen to **Harold,** who tells me, in hindsight, how he may have been trying to penetrate his parents' grief when he chose to write a school book report on Down syndrome in the 5th grade. He tells me, "*My mom was impressed and puzzled by my doing so,*" but missed the chance to comment on the emotional communication encoded in his choosing this topic. Later on, after his brother was institutionalized and **Harold** was made to feel complicit in this, he grew angry. In his anger, he began showing a "*not-so-good son*" side of himself, but even these gestures were missed for their communicative element. Instead, he recalls meeting his parent's admonishments to "*behave better.*" His mother took him for medication in response to his depression. No discussion was had about his feelings, but "*a syrup*" was prescribed to "*help me with the sadness I suppose.*" In one scene, his father damagingly referred to **Harold** as without substance or humaneness. Instead of finding resonance, **Harold's** anger, grief, and confusion were alternatingly met with absence and condemnation. As an adult, **Harold** prefers to observe the impact of pain on other people and has difficultly occupying these parts of his own self-experience.

Darlene grew up alongside her disabled sibling in the home, until her adolescence when her sister was institutionalized. This process broke the dam of dutiful compliance – as she recounts, it felt to her like *"losing her* (sister) *all over again."* She says, *"after she left, [it] was hard for me, and I could not put it on my parents."* The language here is telling because while her sister did not leave of her own volition – it was her parents who institutionalized her sister – Darlene experienced it as a personal abandonment that could not be fully felt in relation to her parents. It also sounds like her adolescent self linguistically speaking its truth. The conflict of not being able to behave in a way that reflected her loss, yet needing to, is made palpable in the way she words the story. She readily identifies with a fear of being left and losing people in the present and tells me that no one in her family at the time *"had the words for it."* The experience itself of institutionalizing a member of the family becomes an "it" experience, a lacuna of trauma. She goes on to tell me how she then attempted to fill the void left by her sister's absence by being the one calling parental attention and worry. *"I became the problem with sexually acting out and other things. I needed parental help regulating myself and soothing myself, but they were not aware or able to provide this."*

When one's troubled dissociated selves are not contained and metabolized by the other, they do not stand much of a chance of being incorporated into a mediated sense of "me"; *"Enmity, aversion, and opposition to the affect states of other parts contribute to the continuing separation of parts"* (Howell, 2016, p. 56). Instead, they exist there behaviorally enacted, accruing shame, and further reifying a need to create dissociative barriers between the parts of self that are acceptable from the parts that are not.

Most survivor siblings do not directly embody or display outwardly their "not me" states among caregivers without a strong event breaking the dam, such as the institutionalization or death of the disabled sibling. **Claire,** whose younger sibling is disabled, describes being caught in the parental web following their divorce and how their differential understating of her brother's condition created collateral damage for her. *"My mom was always criticizing my dad saying he didn't accept my brother's condition."* Instead, both focused on **Claire's** capacities and *"how smart I was."* She was left feeling this was the version of herself she had to deliver:

My mom would assure me that she wasn't kind of pinning all her hopes onto me, and yet she cannot see any deficits in me. For example,

I recall when I was 6 months postpartum and I was telling her I was depressed, and she said, "Oh no, you're just tired."

I include this example as it illustrates the phenomena that can be very much alive and well, dyadically speaking, between survivor siblings and their caregivers, well into adulthood. The psychic demands and wishes for not-me states to be known by entering resonance with attachment figures, as well as the conflict around preserving a parent's sense of having done a good job, may never end.

Absence of a mentalizing dyad or triad

Howell (2016) defines interstate intersubjectivity as "the awareness of the contextual interdependence and interrelatedness of parts of the self that comprise personal depth" (p. 33). She argues that in order for a self-system to be fluid and open, the presence of an "empathic other who could be influenced as well as be influential" is necessary (p. 33). Note the bidirectional nature of the caregiving field as instrumental in promoting this flexibility and developmental adaptation. It is perhaps not surprising, given the lack of mirroring received for negative self-states, that survivor siblings tend to have a lot of difficultly recognizing aggression, as it feels potent and deadly when unmediated. Absent the experience of encountering aggression in dialogue or in the mind of the parent, there is no realm to practice the healthy self-assertion that may come from being in touch with one's own aggression. Separation feels deadly, and so does self-assertion, while being "okay" is a gift one gives routinely to the caregiver. But can you really be "okay" if you are not entitled to boundaries and borders? Aggression is used here as an example, but all kinds of affective experiences that are charged and would threaten the integrity of the familial dissociative structure are left out of the mentalizing dyad or triad. Let's turn our attention here to see how aggression gets thwarted without a containing translator to help in processing it.

Returning to **Harold**, the initial silence surrounding his brother's condition that preceded the betrayal he experienced by his parents institutionalizing his brother without giving him a chance to say goodbye, left **Harold** in a very precarious place. It resulted in what he called a *"tailspin depression,"* and he broke down crying recalling in our interview the only intervention given at the time – a syrup medicine, likely some kind of antidepressant. He goes on to say that it was ultimately the television that intervened. He tells me he watched a documentary about a troubled athlete, which broke his dissociative spell and he sobbed. He did not have parents who could hold his pain in mind, but he found his pain represented in this program and this allowed intermittent contact with his split off grieving and aggrieved self-states. But doing so alone, in a tailspin depression with the television, was not a sustainable encounter that would allow **Harold** to incorporate these experiences into a mediated sense of "me" over time. Instead, he tells me how he routinely feels haunted even up through the present.

Carolyn says:

> *When I went to college, it was intoxicating to be away. I thought for the first time, "is this what it feels like to be happy? Un-burdened?" I think I was very depressed as a kid. Being back with her* [disabled sister] *now, coming back into a primary care role, is depressing. It's not something I'm looking forward to. I'm trying to figure out how I'm going to deal with it emotionally. The ways in which I felt burdened were never attended to by my parents and I am not sure how to do it for myself.*

In this instance, we see how compulsion replaces a more matured capacity to provide care to the self and to others. Absent a mentalizing parent leading the way, Carolyn has had to orchestrate caregiving from the perspective of a younger self without guidance. It's no surprise that for Carolyn this provision of care comes along with dread and self-suppression.

Selena described how her parents' very solid marriage, the *"best bond"* in the family, worked against the provision of a more attuned and specified care to her and her siblings. She elaborates that her mother decided to conceal the cystic fibrosis diagnosis of her disabled sibling from her children, confiding only in her husband and continued to operate in secrecy, even after his premature death. **Selena** could not trust that the closeness her parents offered was ever really the whole story and was left with this unconscious fantasy of having *"stolen all the good things"* from her mother's womb, resulting in her younger sibling's cystic fibrosis disease. *"I protested, why didn't you tell us he was doing to die?"* and her mom replied, *"Oh we thought it was best for you."* But it was not until adulthood that **Selena** understood that her mother, who had become an orphan herself when she was two years old, had repeated the dissociative gap of loss with her own children by failing to imagine the impact of a deceased sibling on them, the way surely no one had imagined her loss as a parentless two-year-old child. She goes on to tell me that her mother, who had passed away last year, never let her deceased sibling go:

My mom had these tape-recording of his [deceased sibling's] *voice, and every time it was his birthday, we'd eat his favorite pastries, and she'd play these tapes. She never let him go – and we were left feeling that we were never ever enough for [her]. We were talking (my surviving brothers and me) – we found in my mom's wardrobe . . . one draw had candies for him, like . . . he was gonna come and take another candy. It was like a museum where time stopped. All his toys . . . part of me was angry, like "let him go mom." She never let him go, something really masochistic, something very sad about that.*

Here we can see how Selena's experience of loss was overshadowed by her mother's grief, and never was met with maternal or paternal recognition. It leaves Selena with more grief than she can bear and no one to help her integrate the deadly aggressive fears and fantasies she held about herself inside.

Darlene was often told of her parents' fairytale love story, in which she, the first-born, figured prominently as desired and wanted. She gives me a before image and an after, by way of her parents, who recounted how freely she danced to live music as a happy one year old in a public setting. When she turned two, and her disabled sister was born, the romanticism gave way to life suddenly absent of any spontaneity. Her parents were worried she'd be made fun of, and they attended to **Darlene's** need to lead a developmentally normal life with a kind of urgency that perhaps crowded out attention to other experiences and may have been driven more by their own wish to return to normalcy. "*My parents were more worried that I'd be made fun of.*" It was *their* spontaneity that had snapped, but it got projected onto her without room for a fuller expression of her experience of this change in family circumstance.

Conclusion

Anxiety, love, and attachment link survivor siblings to their parents – whereas depression, enactive knowing, grief, and absence, link them to their own negated self-states (Chefetz, 2015; Howell, 2016). Without a mediated parental space to work through the latter, these feelings often remain in a dissociative field; there causing havoc internally, but not registered in the space between people in the family in ways that allow for integrative transformation. One way to consider depression is a refusal to go through the process of mourning. Refusal may be too conscious-sounding a word for it. But mourning implies psychic movement whereas depression is stuck and often implies a continued fragmentation of inner self-states. It is frozen, limiting and often enough, a protest in need of translation. Active mourning requires a capacity to be with the multiplicity of self-experience as it unfolds, which the maintenance of dissociative processes foreclose (Dobrich, 2020).

As children, survivor siblings who may have an affective press to mourn given this life experience are not going to be able to engage a process that their caregivers have evaded, and so the motivational system driving attachment may win primacy over the development of a more coherent, inter-systemic self-system and deepening subjectivity. This is known – depression, anxiety, fear, and dissociation work together in tandem, keeping unexperienced-experience at bay or suspended – hanging there as "fact" or "event" but not as experientially accessible. It remains in this unformulated state, not yet encounterable/inhabitable to preserve the bonds within the family and to create homeostasis.

It just may not be possible for the parents living out this legacy to make other allowances for their survivor children. Part of how I envision parents mediating this for their children involves their own capacities to inhabit loss and work it through, which cannot happen in real time before the survivor sibling is going to need those conditions satisfied in their parents because they are all sharing the same relational landscape in real time. None of us can offer to others what remains undone in ourselves even though we may wish this were possible. I cannot solve the difficulty here except to echo Boss' (1999) recognition that dialectical experiencing both within the self and between each other is how to optimally move through ambiguous loss. And if the caregiving system cannot initially or sequentially do so, having other attachment figures to turn to for survivor siblings is really important.

Hopenwasser (2008) uses the term dissociative attunement to capture the "physics of resonance and the biology of entrainment" that accompany the process of synching up experience affectively together (p. 354). Importantly she notes, the sync-up can lead to healing or re-traumatization, as the synching alone does not define on what frequency the people will join.

This is why the relational phenomena that happen between survivor siblings and their caregivers are the same phenomena that are encountered transferentially and counter-transferentially within the treatment dyad later on, and with varying results. Initial sync-ups may mean resonating without touching on the dissociative content that ultimately will need to make its way into the therapeutic field gradually overtime in ways that did not happen during childhood itself. Without the third space a mediated psychoanalytic treatment affords, these buried inner selves become more and more desperate to be heard over the course of development, which leads to an unholy inner experience of chaos that can cause affective disruptions in living. These disavowed self-states often continue to remain outside the space of recognition within the early caregiving relationship well into adulthood. But dissociative awakenings come to survivors in many forms throughout life. And as will be discussed in the next chapter, opportunities to awaken to dissociative process can occur not only through the familiar medium of being a patient but also within vocational callings, such as the desire to become a psychoanalyst.

Notes

1 As I was revising this manuscript, I saw the Broadway Show *Jagged Little Pill* and was delighted to encounter a semi-primary character represent the plight of survivor siblings. The surprise registered for me, how unusual it is to see representations of a survivor sibling's perspective.
2 I'm using split off here to denote the parts of the self that are actively 'not' shared with the caregivers, and necessarily not recognized internally. So for example, survivor sibs oriented toward understanding absence have contact with this part of themselves, but it does not enter into the mediated intersubjective space between them and their caregivers.

References

Batshaw, M., Pellegrino L., & Roizen, N. (Eds.). (2007). *Children with disabilities* (6th ed.). Brookes.
Bion, W. R. (1962). *Learning from experience*. Tavistock.
Boss, P. (1999). *Ambiguous loss: Learning to live with unresolved grief*. Harvard University Press.
Bromberg, P. M. (1996). Standing in the spaces: The multiplicity of self and the psychoanalytic relationship. *Contemporary Psychoanalysis, 32*, 509–535.
Bromberg, P. M. (1998). *Standing in the spaces: Essays on clinical process*. Psychology Press.
Chefetz, R. (2015). *Intensive psychotherapy for persistent dissociative processes: The fear of feeling real*. W. W. Norton Company.
Crastonopol, M. (2015). *Micro trauma: A psychoanalytic understanding of cumulative psychic trauma*. Routledge.

Dobrich, J. (2020). An elegy for motherless daughters: Multiplicity, mourning & dissociation. *Psychoanalytic Perspectives, 17*(3), 366–384,

Fairbairn, W. D. (1963). Synopsis of an object-relations theory of the personality. *International Journal of Psycho-Analysis, 44*, 224–225.

Ferenczi, S. (1949). Confusion of the tongues between the adults and the child: The language of tenderness and of passion. *International Journal of Psycho-Analysis, 30*, 225–230.

Hopenwasser, K. (2008). Being in rhythm: Dissociative attunement in therapeutic process. *Journal of Trauma & Dissociation, 9*(3), 349–367.

Hopenwasser, K. (2018). Bearing the unbearable: Meditations on being in rhythm. *Attachment: New Directions in Psychotherapy and Relational Psychoanalysis, 12*(1), 48–55.

Howell, E. (2016). *The dissociative mind in psychoanalysis: Understanding and working with trauma.* Routledge.

Kingsley, E. P. (1987). *Welcome to Holland.* www.dsasc.ca/uploads/8/5/3/9/8539131/welcome_to_holland.pdf

Lyons-Ruth, K., Dutra, L., Schuder, M. & Bianchi, I. (2006). From infant attachment disorganization to adult dissociation: Relational adaptations or traumatic experiences? *Psychiatric Clinics of North America, 29*(1), 63–86.

Putnam, F. (2016). *The way we are: How states of mind influence our identities, personality and potential for change.* International Psychoanalytic Books.

Schore, A. N. (2009). Attachment trauma and the developing right brain: Origins of pathological dissociation. In P. F. Dell & J. A. O'Neil (Eds.), *Dissociation and the dissociative disorders: DSM-V and beyond* (pp. 107–141). Routledge.

Siegel, D. J. (2012). *The developing mind: How relationships and the brain interact to shape who we are* (2nd ed.). Guilford Press.

Solomon, A. (2012). *Far from the tree: Parents, children & the search for identity.* Scribner Simon & Schuster.

Stern, S. (2019). Airless worlds: The traumatic sequelae of identification with parental negation. *Psychoanalytic Dialogues, 29*, 435–450.

Van der Hart, O., Nijenhuis, E., & Steele, K. (2006). *The haunted self: Structural dissociation and the treatment of chronic traumatization.* W. W. Norton Company.

Vargas, C. M., & Prelock, P. A. (Eds.). (2004). *Caring for children with neurodevelopmental disabilities and their families: An innovative approach to interdisciplinary practice.* Lawrence Erlbaum Associates.

Winnicott, D. W. (1965). *The maturational processes and the facilitating environment: Studies in the theory of emotional development.* Hogarth Press and the Institute of Psychoanalysis.

Chapter 5

Answering the call to heal

During my first year of college, I sat alongside my mother, father and other survivor sibling in the audience at the institutional facility where my brother now lives. It had only been about a year since my disabled brother was placed and for the first time living outside our family home. The secondary trauma surrounding his institutionalization – the medical crises it caused him from the adverse reaction to the surgical insertion of the feeding tube, the unraveling of my parents' alliance after a shared lifetime of devotion and care provided to him, and the shock of his being sent away – all reverberated around me at the time thick as smoke, choking out any possibility of containment or joy, in tandem with the cigarettes I secretly then smoked. I was not alone; I could feel the fragility of everyone's feelings around me too. But these were not things that we discussed directly. I watched as my father withdrew into depression, my mother her work, as me and my other brother tried to go on living like things were "normal," further dissociating parts of our self-experience to make this possible. It was nearly Christmas and we sat at the institutional winter holiday show.

Have you ever been to an institutional setting? It is filled with children of varying ages and capacities that all have severe enough conditions to merit lifetime placement. As the lights dimmed a group of six wheel-chaired kids occupied the stage, pushed by volunteer dancers. Music began to fill the auditorium with the words of Lee Ann Womack:

> I hope you never lose your sense of wonder
> You get your fill to eat but always keep that hunger
> May you never take one single breath for granted
> God forbid love ever leave you empty handed . . .
> Promise me that you'll give faith a fighting chance

And when you get the choice to sit it out or dance
I hope you dance

I was grateful to the dark for concealing the tears that steadily streamed down my cheeks.

I regret writing what follows, as I imagine my readers will think I was identified with the kids in wheelchairs on the stage and that my tears represented my being moved by this moment. But it was not the kids on stage whose feelings I felt in this moment. Instead, a fury rose inside me along with an internal monologue that went something like this. . .

Of all songs! Sit it out or dance?! Fill the hunger? With what, nutritional liquid for the feeding tubes? Are they kidding me? Why? Are we really going to Pollyanna this experience too? Turn our family's current tragedy into triumph? Who's triumphant here? The social workers and dance therapists who stroll in on legs that walk to wheel around the wheelchair bound and often brain damaged kids so they can put it on their resumes and get into good graduate programs before they head home for the holiday? Ugh. What is everyone else thinking? I bet this audience is eating this up. Kill me now.

Secretly harboring such un-generous thoughts and feelings, while this anger overlay the enormous grief I could not get to experience in relation to others at knowing my brother would never dance on his own, or get up and live an autonomous life outside the institution, left me feeling monstrous. I knew there were other ways to experience this event, and perhaps other parts of me had a different take on this same scene. I also knew that some of the disabled children themselves were benefiting from this creative arts program and did feel they could dance. For all I knew, these children may have even been the ones to select the chosen song. But because the reality of my brother's limitations had been placed in an affective "off-limits" category given my family's survival strategies, I could not hold the contradiction made possible in hearing the song as metaphor long enough to stomach the hypocrisy. The fact was that most of these children and their families would not dance or live lives full of gratitude for their fortunes. At the time, the suggestion that they ought to or that we, as their families, ought to feel the presence of God's investment in them and in us, made me furious. But I told no one this. When the show ended, we remarked to one another on the things we could stomach – "such a great auditorium," "what a beautiful facility," and "what a nice way to bring people together."

It is one of the moments that haunt me because it illustrates all the negative space of a dissociative process. So much feeling remains inside of me that is not able to get experienced in relationship to another, including even a more reflective part of myself. I am, of course, also haunted by the idea of displaying this judgmental, nonpolitically correct, irate self-state to you, the readers. But breaking up my own dissociative silos around my brother's condition and its actual impact on our family life and my own identity is, in large part, what led me to become a psychoanalyst – although implying it was a conscious motivation may be misleading because my experience of survivorship was unformulated growing up and into young adulthood (Stern, 1983, 2019). If I had told a story that flatters me here, I'd be doing more of the same make-believe that characterizes a lot of *as-if* living and as noted earlier sustains the insecure/disorganized attachment system between survivor siblings and parents.

Psychoanalysis as a facilitative environment

Somehow as a child I developed an impression that psychoanalysis was the place where people went to tell the truth about their inner most selves. I do not know how I knew this. Maybe it was an artifact of the complicated relationship with my mom, herself a developmental psychologist and clinician, and her deep distrust of Freud that led me to fantasize that he was the Father I needed to find my way back to myself/ves? As I grew up and read on my own, psychoanalysis seemed to be the place where self-censorship was respected for the defensive functions it served, but ultimately dismantled, as an analytic encounter was meant to liberate the subjective truth of a life (or lives). And it was the only place I could imagine where my own dissociative contradictions could be met with what I naively then interpreted as Freud's sympathy. Later it came as a devastation to realize he would have blamed my "hysteria" on fantasy rather than lived reality, but that's for a different book. Of course, I did not know this consciously, so it sounds strange to write in this way. Stern (1983) defines unformulated experience as:

> The perceptions, ideas, and memories we prefer not to have, the observations we prefer not to make, are most often murky and poorly defined, different in kind than they will be when the process of completion has progressed to the level of words.

(p. 71)

To know about one's own unconscious motivations in becoming a psychoanalyst engages the process of moving unformulated experience into a verbal and ultimately linguistic realm. Most interviewees inhabit this process underlying the relationship between their survivorship and practicing psychoanalysis like the peeling away of an onion or those Russian nesting dolls that sit inside one another. There is seemingly no end to the stripping away or the hidden inner self-states experience of why you thought you were doing this.

I want to be careful here not to dichotomize the calling. While it is my perspective that it is informed by both traumatic constriction and excess, it is not necessarily pathologically driven nor can it be entirely altruistic. And while it is often a good natural fit because of these autobiographical experiences with survivorship, I think what ultimately drives the calling for many of us is a semiconscious or unconscious attempt to get at the unexperienced-experience from the other side of the couch. The degree to which it is "good" or "bad" is misleading; I ask instead, whether it's facilitative. Boss (1999) writes:

> Ambiguous loss is devastating and can have lasting traumatic effects. But with support and resilience some people use the experience to learn how to live in difficult circumstances throughout life, balancing the ability to grieve what was lost with the recognition of what is still possible.
>
> (p. 135)

The practice of psychoanalysis embraces paradox and contradiction as core human experiences that (hopefully) evolve within a developmental context (Pizer, 1992; Winnicott, 1951, 1958), one such paradox being that to move forward one must go backward – or put differently, that growth requires mourning. Practicing the active presence required in being a psychoanalyst is an act of devotion, to the self and to the people whom one treats, whether one knows it or not.

Glimmers of knowing: dissociation versus repression

The relationship between survivorship and the vocational choice of becoming someone whose job it is to listen with exquisite sensitivity to human experience evolves for all of us, over time. But how does this work? I want to argue that doing the clinical work itself is a vital part of the evolutionary process in consciousness because it provides a context in which such knowings develop and mature. This requires breaking up the hegemony of the intrapsychic structural model that places repression at the core of human experience. Most analysts agree that knowing and taking personal responsibility for what drives the calling is necessary for the optimization of the analytic process, and many a training analysis begins in this territory. Analytic views that place a premium on repression as the basic building block of human intrapsychic structure assume that for an analyst *not to know* is to not fully engage (one's) resistance. For example, Sussman (1992) writes that the unconscious motivations of the analyst "are what have brought the therapist into the relationship with the patient and they will inevitably shape all subsequent interactions" (p. 7). Sussman's perspective implies that remaining unconsciously driven to heal oneself may act as a kind of treatment interference. Curative fantasies of the analyst may live in the unconscious, but structurally, where one places unconscious experience – and its relationship to consciousness – has implications. For example, Schaffer (2006) writes:

> becoming an analyst requires careful attention to one's personal equation. This includes knowing the motivations that brought one into the field and the ways these continue to find expression in one's sense of what is curative.
>
> (p. 364)

In both these formulations, unconscious motivations remain repressed as opposed to dissociated, as each author implies exploration of the unconscious motivations is a prerequisite to the work or at least co-occurring, ideally with the analyst ahead of the patient in this regard. The mechanism by which repressed material is made accessible is different than dissociated material, whose form requires by definition a not-knowing encounter, as opposed to a left-brain exposition, to become formulated in the first place.

Approaching the question of survivorship from a structural model of dissociation means our curative fantasies and motivations for becoming therapists, more than likely, exist in the realm of unformulated experience and across different self-states, with varying degrees of awareness held at any given time and in any given context. The split is not between conscious and unconscious experience itself but instead across self-states, each of which houses conscious and unconscious experience, some states of which may more fully know what's being activated in them and why. It is not possible to arrive into a definitive state of knowing fully and taking complete responsibility for one's inner motivations, in the way it is fantasized that insight works with repression. Instead, a structural dissociation model implies the presence of absence – that is, experience not fully entered into or even there to be pushed down by repressive forces to begin with. It follows that consciousness regarding unconscious motivations may arrive from any durable encounter that gives survivors access to this realm of unexperienced-experience along with a mediating third position from which to see it, but by definition cannot be known before then or gotten from analyzing the experience itself, a priori. For example, it is not uncommon to hear survivor siblings discuss their clinical work with severely disturbed patients who they may treat initially without any awareness of their own survivorship until self-analysis or colleague supervision leads one to realize the work invites them to enter into the relational experience of being the intact sibling and other relational configurations that follow. Listen to Perlman (1999), a survivor sibling analyst, describe this in his own words:

> As I sit waiting for my patient, my stomach feels edgy and my teeth are clenched. . . . What emerges is a recurrent childhood dream familiar from my own psychotherapy: My younger sister is falling into a dark, bottomless well, probably to her death. . . . I'm holding her hand with all my might but she is slipping away. I wake up distraught. The patient's message (of threatening suicide) feels like the relationship with my sister in the dream. One of my sorrows is that I could not save my sister and that inability is part of my motivation in treating traumatized and abused patients. I realize that I am confusing my patient with my sister. This is a relief. I continue exploring. Each of these patients is in part my sister to me. I knew this before but, had forgotten it. Each patient I treat is some penance for not saving her. This is a new realization.
>
> (pp. xi–xii)

What sets Perlman entering into a state of knowing is first the recognition of somatic discomfort, followed by an experience of terror that he is then able to mentalize, importantly, in the context of a dyad where he has his patient's presence operative. In doing so, he realizes that he knows this fear in some place of him, some other self-state held some glimmer of knowledge, but we can assume it was unintegrated as he explains how he "forgot." If enactments are the "interpersonalization of dissociation," the dissociated experience of survivorship gets encountered in the clinical experience as much as by parts of the analyst as by the self-states of their patients – and both "sides" of the dyad are needed to translate the dissociated content (Stern, 2004). Whether a model of repression or dissociation is centered, there is no such thing as being fully analyzed and completely aware of one's unconscious curative fantasies. But I am also saying that with dissociation, unconsciously engaging in the clinical work itself becomes the arena in which dissociative unformulated process is made manifest.

I realize that models which center and assume repression as the pivotal defining feature of unconscious life are not saying that one has to totally know their own unconscious – by definition, that's not possible. But there is a different sensibility engaged when someone writes from a dissociative model as opposed to a repressive one. To me, it is a felt-sense. Trying to put it to words, I'd say the relationship between conscious and unconscious experience is approached very differently. There is a felt sense of respect for experience that is uninhabited and a danger to the homeostasis of a self-system that I feel too often is evaded in models that assume repression is at work. There is good reason to *not know* everything and in my opinion, this does not mean one is necessarily disabled from performing the role of clinician or doing a disservice to the patient. One's attitude toward what they do not know differentiates readiness for clinical work. A capacity to tolerate shame, which always accompanies absence and gaps in awareness, is necessary, but the insight itself is not. Dissociative models place an emphasis on *being-with*, not knowing or insight. One can paradoxically find out what they need to know by first inhabiting the experience of being with another, right brain to right brain (DeYoung, 2015). Accumulated over time, these experiences of being with patients result in expanded consciousness regarding the relationship between survivorship and the work.

Schaffer (2006) illustrates how supervision may become instrumental in helping analysts come to know their inner fantasies related to cure by providing a mediatory space. You can become a therapist without necessarily knowing how this autobiographical experience will be with you in the room in real time, but once you are that therapist with the right support, your clinical work gives you many opportunities to enliven and inhabit unexperienced-experience. So for many interviewees, myself included, there is a felt possibility, if unarticulated as such, of (self) integration and inhabitation, that goes along with becoming an analyst. There is a sense that the inhabitation of self-states generated and maintained through survivorship goes along with doing the work; it is the only job I can think of where it is not only okay to do so but also necessary. Consciously, the motivation to become a therapist may first sound like (or be about) healing the Other. But underneath, intrapsychically speaking, there may be no distinction between the Other and the Self, as the disabled sibling and parent/s all form, constrain, and shape the subjectivity of the survivor sibling. To save others is to save oneself, and vice versa.

So if we look at the question regarding the fate of an analyst's wounds from a place of dissociation, as opposed to resistance or repression, it is not the unthought-known but the unexperienced-experience that may be sought out through the analytic encounter (Bollas, 1987). What better place is there to find frozen/unintegrated experiences than in the intimacy and immediacy of the therapeutic relationship, which sets the stage for dramatic dialogue to unfold (Atlas & Aron, 2018)? A truly intersubjective model will necessarily break down the distinction between analyst and patient, making the question of how to inhabit one's messy subjectivity the cornerstone of the encounter. Harris (2009) writes,

> we need to see the inevitable presence in the analyst of wounds that must serve as tools, aspects of the analyst's capacities that are simultaneously brakes on and potentials for change . . . expressed through a commitment to the inevitable immersion in enactment and the living with one's own toxicity as well as the patient's.
>
> (p. 5)

That said, I do not think that all states of awareness regarding self-knowledge about wounds offer equal opportunities for therapeutic healing. If this were so, what would be the purpose of training and practicing? But I guess I want to demystify the notion that we can ever fully grasp our curative fantasies and mature out of them, while at the same time, saying the way we become better analysts requires paradoxically a chance to live them out in process again and again, with different awareness each time. While many survivor siblings are initially somewhat conscious of their motivation to offset guilt through caretaking and advocacy of others, it seems to take layers of doing clinical work and experience to recognize how this vocational choice may also be serving a wish to heal one's own vulnerable, unmirrored inner selves which can only come about through integrative contact with the unexperienced-experience. This can be done from both sides of the couch, really. Many times during an interview between the author and a subject, something new would be felt and learned by us both about how this sibling experience is with us "in the room" as both patients and clinicians. The third space of supervision itself was also found to be a very illuminating and mediatory space, as analysts mature into building and sustaining this space internally.

The subjective experience of the analyst

Being a psychoanalyst means meeting each moment internally with as much subjective honesty as one can muster, always knowing that the relationship between consciousness and unconsciousness is never fully knowable by any of us (Stern, 2019). Holding close to heart what we know to be valuable from our histories and analyses allows us to be present in an honest way for our patients and for ourselves. If we consider that what we do is informed by all the experiences we've encountered which shape who and how we are in the world and within ourselves, and want our patients to think similarly along these lines, from an inter-subjective standpoint, it is important to examine the relationship between personal experience and vocational leanings, not as a static point in time, but something that evolves as we grow and find more (inner) room to know about it. Any experience and the depth to which it is encountered or evaded can serve more than one master at a time, and consciousness may only hold some of that awareness in mind.

The advent of relational psychoanalysis has made exploring this relationship between personal analytic subjectivity and clinical work relevant in a way that prior notions of psychoanalysis could not (Farber, 2017; Gerson, 1996; Harris, 2009; Kuchuck, 2014). Rather than view it as navel gazing or acting out, the end of the one-person regime ushered in the possibility of understanding the analyst's subjectivity as directly relevant to what can and cannot transpire in the clinical encounter. In describing his professional voyage from an orientation of classical psychoanalysis to relational psychoanalysis, Kuchuck (2014) writes how the trauma of 9/11 accelerated his evolutionary process:

> This book, then, is borne of the storming in of my own and the profession's subjectivity . . . it is a collection that celebrates an emergence from hiding on the parts of authors, analysts, and a profession.
>
> (p. xxiv)

The interest in the personal lives of psychoanalysts is finally rooted in the understanding that the subjectivity of both participants in an analytic encounter informs the process. Farber (2017) writes, "today, relational theory believes all feelings, thoughts, and actions of both patient and analyst are embedded in an intersubjective field" (p. 7). In the literature, a good deal of attention is now paid to the impact of early object loss, and other character-informing events, as precipitating factors informing the motivation to become a "wounded healer" (Barnett, 2007; Farber, 2017; Gerson, 1996; Harris, 2009; Kuchuck, 2014). The analyst's curative fantasies and their relationship to clinical work as they get enacted relationally over time are considered a valuable subject (Schaffer, 2006). Where these wounds were once viewed as liability and an indicator of one not being thoroughly analyzed or a deficit in self-awareness, the room for unformulated experience is thankfully better understood (Stern, 1983, 2019). The analyst's use of their own dissociative experience within the treatment – not just attending to whatever a patient is repeating (as was a one-person perspective on this) – in contemporary times is widely considered a vehicle for therapeutic action. A healer's relational wounds are now understood as source data, implicated in the kinds of capacities and pitfalls made possible in interaction within the analytic relationship, as opposed to unconscious blocks. The fate of these wounds within the healer are not predetermined, nor are they static.

I hope this chapter encourages readers to consider the sibling dimension as yet another prospective variable informing one's calling to practice psychoanalysis in its own right, independent of the much more familiar wish to cure one's parents. More specifically, I hope to tie the notion of unexperienced-experience, and the drive to find a context for embodiment and encountering, at the heart of what motivates many survivor siblings toward this work, wherever they may be along the continuum of knowing this to be so. Mourning paradoxically is both solitary and relational at once; you need both dimensions to mourn. Every analytic encounter prospectively offers a specific relational context to mourn. I am sure there is a destination beyond even the recognition of healing one's inner fractured/damaged selves that I do not yet see connected to this calling. All "stages" of consciousness described are like Ogden's transformation of Melanie Klein's positions; they are not developmentally outgrown, but instead held in dialectical tension (Klein, 1940; Ogden, 1989). Let's take a look and see what the survivor siblings have to say about their shifting self-knowledge regarding the call to heal as it gets formulated through experience, time, and clinical interaction.

To be of service, to assuage guilt, and to make contact with the missing other

The first layer of the onion in consciousness regarding being a therapist involves assuaging a sense of survivor's guilt. Of survivor guilt, psychoanalyst and writer Jeanne Safer (2002) articulates:

> Guilt is rarely absent from the thoughts of healthy adults about their damaged siblings. . . . Whether they embrace caretaking as a mission or categorically refuse it. . . [these] siblings . . . are forced by accidents of fate to deal with a dilemma that nobody else has to think about.
>
> (p. 140)

Because some degree of the guilt of surviving is usually conscious, it is not uncommon for survivor siblings to know something about how this guilt motivates them toward caretaking. Caplan (2011), who conducted the first empirical study of survivor siblings in a campus counseling setting, describes:

> Loyalty, the wish to help, guilt and shame can influence the process of developing a vocational identity, either drawing students to or inhibiting them from pursuing particular interests . . . with the most obvious choice . . . the helping professions.
>
> (p. 126)

By design, I was most likely to talk to the subjects who were drawn toward caretaking, as being a psychoanalyst was a condition that had to be met to be in the sample, though both quotes illustrate that moving away from caretaking is an equally viable possibility – identification and dis-identification with caretaking, being two sides of the same coin. In talking with the participants of my study, all subjects confirmed that listening in a deep way to others, particularly others in distress from outside the family, came naturally as a result of their lived experience within the family. When feelings of guilt about their abledness are evoked in the work, survivor siblings typically find it easier to bear and to analyze self-reflectively than they once did in the original family situation. This guilt related to having capacities is connected to the parts of self that do not experience their lack. Attending to others becomes a reflexive, habituated process that does not distinguish a listening stance of presence from one of performance. Bowlby's classification of children who "tend and befriend" precociously as a relational strategy in an insecure attachment system and Winnicott's "false self" come readily to mind here (Bowlby, 1960; Winnicott, 1965). Reflexive behavior by definition is not informed by self-analysis. Compulsive helping is not the same thing as embodied witnessing, but how does one get from one place to the other?

I think the answer comes from the second point Caplan (2011) identifies. The dawning sensation that something within the analyst-self is settled or comforted by giving back to others in need, opens a portal for some to be/come curious about what needs settling in themselves – the burgeoning of self-awareness regarding aspects of motivation that were previously hidden within a dissociative fog. It brings reflexive behavior into the space of curiosity and introspection. Only then can one encounter and work with their feelings of guilt and helplessness directly (in self-supervision or supervision with others) as many patients (thankfully) do not respond well to an analyst using the treatment for their own guilt-assuaging needs particularly if they remain wholly unconscious. For those patients that do stay, the enactment driven by analysts' unreflective need to assuage their own guilt likely creates an impasse of possibility for greater awareness to come in. Harris (2009) describes how impasse is an opportunity for an analyst to drop their habituated use of omnipotence and instead to grieve. She writes:

> The task of distinguishing clinical responsibility from omnipotence is endless and exacting and always, to some degree, indeterminate. It is never solely the problem of sorting the origins of affect but also bearing the personal affective states, with all their personal historical force, in us.

(p. 9)

In what follows, you can hear the burgeoning sense of awareness regarding the survivor siblings' psychic need to "help," either by making reparation and/or sustaining contact with the missing other/s:

Natalie: The condition of my sister was decisive in the choice of my profession. I was aware of it from the moment I made the decision to study psychology . . . I wanted to help people with their suffering because somehow I connected easily with their pain. Mainly, I am interested in knowing how it is for a mother to have a sick and disabled child.

Harold: I didn't have support or encouragement earlier in life when I expressed interest in becoming a psychotherapist, but I always had this early calling to listen despite the interference of structural circumstances. I guess it's an extension of the wish to be helpful, and to discover more about myself, to help myself and to make myself more effective with other people. . . . The carrying around of patients in your head 24/7 seems like a great preoccupation and tonic.

Susan: I was a social worker for a long time and driven by a social justice imperative. I worked in education, but over many years came to see that organizing social action alone does not get at the core of where people change, so my interest morphed from healing empowerment, to healing to change. My sister taught me how to trust communicating non-verbally, which also made a therapist role naturally fitting.

Hannah: My decision to be an analyst was very related to both my differently disabled brothers. But as I always tell others, people become therapists either to help or to harm. I think I was always trying to help my mom and brothers by attempting to understand why people do what they do, and how they become who they are. I received a command to go to social work school during meditation. Analytic training followed, and it was the coolest thing I've ever done. It gave me a way to understand my inherited family dynamics. I really wanted to help, and felt I had taken so much already in my selfish life, I wanted to give back.

Kira: I initially went into advertising, but found myself working alongside an investigation about a clean needle injection site. I should have known then that I cared more about human suffering than products! I was a very aware little child, I had empathy and guilt toward my sister, I saw my parents helping others and modeling sacrifice so it became embedded in me. I never saw my parents complain. We never took a vacation but never did they lament this. I adopted this, so even on the days when I was tired, I found a sense of pride and purpose in looking after my sister. I also had so much exposure to the medical world that caring for others seemed a natural fit. These things informed my becoming a therapist in ways I am still learning about.

In each illustration, we hear how the drive to help others feels emotionally tied to helping the self, but mostly implicitly. Consciously what is sought is a recovered lost other. This level of awareness can be seen as an effort to locate experientially what is lost; that being with others in pain will put them in touch with their own inner objects, an enactment of the searching for the lost Other(s). The focus is on making contact with the sibling or bereft parents as the focal point of awareness. Each account also shows the subject's fantasy of how the therapeutic space would allow for a deepened engagement. A more nuanced grasp of the contradictions and hidden wishes of parts of self may not be explicit yet, but the pull toward finding a resonant environment remains alive in each of these examples. Given the absence of a sustained mediatory environment during development, it is remarkable that survivor siblings allow themselves to dream it up or to find it later on, through this vocational choice.

Between my sibling and my-selves

As we talked further and as a subject would veer toward saying they could not or did not treat people who were physically disabled or "like their sibling" in a concrete sense, we came to realize more fully the personal significance represented by their imagined patients and the tie to their own wounded healer fantasy (Farber, 2017). In other words, it was not their sibling in fantasy per se that they were treating, or even their parents, a common psychoanalytic reference point for most in the profession, but instead themselves. In particular, being an analyst engaged those self-states that never entered into the mirroring resonance with caregivers or the rest of the self-system and for whom an integrative healing environment was necessary.

Olina: I am sure the sibling experience was a part of my decision but I don't know if I was conscious of it. I had already been in therapy for a while before considering becoming one myself. I knew about my family role as caretaker of other's emotions and needs. By necessity I'd been good at listening to other people and sensing what they needed. My first internship was in foster care, and I remember this young girl client would take things from my office and I resonated with her, her need to take. Though I wrote my thesis of course on "giving," what does it mean to give? I was grappling with these questions internally. Bodily experience intruded as I dealt with IBS, and noticed my posture was always folding in on itself.

Carolyn: I was conscious of the link here immediately . . . and it was directly related to my living with my disabled sibling and to an awareness of how much pain needed to be addressed. This awareness of dynamics going on and no one noticing, internal worlds happening, including my own, was the main thing propelling me forward in the career. It wasn't until college though that I really found my own pain . . . being away from the family for the first time. As the healer now, I am forced to deal with it finally.

Rose: It was not consciously connected. In graduate school it dawned on me that I'm in this club of people who had to take care of their parents, the emotional caretakers. I immediately resonated with that aspect of entering the healing professions, but it took longer to get to my sibling experience. A big part for me was feeling I didn't deserve to have a good life, because I got what my sister didn't have. I imagined her life was shitty and so unconsciously for all these years I did not allow myself to have much of a life, in big ways. All this led to a big capacity for empathy – I can sit with people in pain, can hold it well.

Claire: Well, I landed here as a combination of both of my parents' skills. My mom is a social worker. Leaning toward psychoanalysis is a move away from her. I never had an interest in treating disabled people or doing the kind of concrete care she does. I have worked with kids but not with disabilities, just feel that I've had enough of that in my lifetime. I think I am here for me.

Debra: It's really complicated to name the relationship between my vocation and life experience because there is a limit to what I know I know. I am sure it is related to my sister, and more than that too. A really important figure on my mom's side of the family had been a psychoanalyst, and this identification definitely unconsciously contributed to my leanings.

This level of awareness included realizing more directly how the wounded healer is driven to heal thyself, as opposed to being of service habitually to the disabled sibling or forlorn parents. While not fully embracing the vantage point of recognizing one's not-mes, these remarks show the subtle transition away from the earlier omnipotent self's wish to help my-sibling/ parents as they move more explicitly into the terrain of doing this work is beyond my sibling/parents, though not yet explicitly for the buried inner selves. A degree of differentiation from earlier modes of survival can be heard in these sorts of reflections. The compulsive caretaking is questioned, and restricted, not on offer all the time for anyone, and perhaps also less driven by a need to secure the right to exist. Wandering in these inner waters brings about the possibility for contacting one's grief at not having, rather than offloading the sense of having unconsciously through forced feeds. The beginnings of entering and inhabiting the unexperienced-experience in a meditative, as opposed to a reactive, fashion ripen under such know-ings. But just to be clear, the bridge here requires enacting omnipotent rescue fantasies first because only by enlivening these states can we come to see them and own them. Just like we continue to need the autistic-con-tiguous, paranoid-schizoid, and depressive positions of relationality, we oscillate in and out of these varying levels of awareness and motivations in being clinicians (Ogden, 1989).

Healing hidden/unrelated inner selves

Identified with psychic pain, silence, and the invisible kind of suffering dissociative processes invite, many survivor siblings describe feeling they were initially drawn to psychoanalysis to witness others, and as they advance in experience and age, come to find out that doing so requires encountering aspects of their own experience that have been untouched or left in a (semi) dissociative state, in whatever way accommodating the family narrative around disability required of them. In reaching a place of dissociative attunement with patients, survivor siblings are drawn into the very spaces for which they lacked resonance during development (Hopen-wasser, 2008). This encountering can be brought on through the experience of being a patient or being the analyst. In addition to being motivated by fantasies of bringing healing and connection to their parents and disabled sibling(s), over time and practice, comes a deepening and steady aware-ness of how one's own dissociated states are ultimately engaged with in reverie and interaction, in ways that were previously foreclosed, generated by the very longing to provide this experience to one's patients. These not-me states come into sharper experiential focus during clinical encounters and are thereafter, more consciously present.

At this stage, consciousness is more fully brought to how the clinical experience is altering the interior experience of the survivor siblings them-selves, by placing them within unexperienced-experience.

Marisa: Well, it was certainly not a conscious choice but I think I gravi-tated here because I was anxious and depressed. I remember a career day event in school and hearing a therapist speak . . . as soon as I understood therapists attended to people suffering from emotional pain- and not physical pain, I thought, that's for me! That's me! Physical pain belonged to my sister, but emotional suffering was mine. Of course we each had both, but the idea of being a therapist was about being with people like myself, who had a need to be met and my wanting to meet it, and have it met for myself, really stirred the motivations in me.

Darlene: I became conscious of the connection between my experience and becoming a therapist during my own first treatment. As I'd try to put words to experiences and memories, for which there had not been any words before. As I was doing it, it seemed like a perfect fit for me. To be with people as they start to put words around their unnamed and unacknowledged experiences. I found I was not easily shocked by the full range of fantasies people have about their parents and their siblings, I had them too, and recognized them.

Rachel: Back in the throes of the chaos growing up, I could only meet my sister in this regressive place, and so I was exposed to the helping professions myself when I was young and grew comfortable with the idea that when you struggle, there can be professionals there to help. As my anxiety got more pro-nounced in high school and college, I came to rely on my aunt surrogate's perspective and advice. But I never wanted to work with kids or the disabled. I went to psychoanalysis to get away from my sister. I differentiated from her by choosing this profession and was really drawn to it, when I felt what it had to offer me.

Selena: Being a psychoanalyst is the gift I got from this autobiographical experience. It was funny because I didn't know – in one way, you know your story, your body, your feelings, but it was not clear to me in words this relationship between life circumstance, and the profession. I consciously decided to study psychology as an undergraduate because I thought I'd have value if I could help, and it helped me to feel that I have something good for people. Ultimately my first job was working in a children's hospital always around death, seeking to make reparation. Years later, I understood why I was so interested in that, for myself. Then well, my career, my profession was the good thing about this experience, without knowing then what led me here. My other brother became a priest, a healer of guilty souls, while I healed emotional lives, and you can't help but heal your own as you go along.

These illustrations show survivor siblings reckoning with their own psychic needs in the process of becoming and doing psychoanalytic work. It is not the absence of their sibling or their parents in the curative fantasies, but the presence of their own inner (neglected) selves that mark the distinction between this level of awareness and the others described. We hear how these analysts are able to utilize the clinical encounter to enter into their own unexperienced-experience and reach the realm of what remains unformulated in a more reflective rather than reactive spirit. Stern (1983) captures this stance as he writes:

We cannot force formulation. We can only prepare ourselves by immersion in our field of interest and then remain open to possibility, seizing it (attending to it) whenever it appears. It is not enough to "put our backs into" the forging of new formulations, though we must be willing to do this when the time comes and the vague outlines of something new begin to emerge.

(p. 89)

Remaining open to experience is not a mindset, but a sensibility. There's no limit to what analysts are asked to hold on behalf of their patients and themselves in the service of formulation and may include such difficult feelings as inadequacy, shame, worthlessness, lust, fury, dependency, or resignation. Sometimes it's our patients who get to their unformulated dissociative silos first, and we realize in accompanying them that we can and will have to enter too. Other times, we arrive first at knowing inner parts that have been ailing in silence cut off from the rest of ourselves that make this possibility come alive for the patient. Farber (2017) writes:

> as we come to identify and accept our own inner woundedness and can empathize more fully with the patient, the experience changes us as healers as much as it changes the patient.
>
> (p. 48)

Conclusion

Taken together, these reflections offer a snapshot of an awareness that remains in process and is necessarily incomplete and always evolving. Our understanding of things is always in motion. While it may be the wounds themselves that drive one toward the practice of psychoanalysis, one's faith and commitment to knowing about them, to learning how to inhabit them, sometimes for the first time ever, mark the distinction between traumatic repetition and something new becoming possible. In order to appreciate the differing levels of awareness regarding the vocational calling and it's relation to one's recognition of their autobiographical experience, we'll now turn to the place in which many such knowings are born. Tessman (2003) writes,

> Our theories have long held that identification with the analyst and his or her analytic function is the cornerstone for building one's own analytic capacities, just as we have long believed that a good identification with the parents is needed for healthy development.
>
> (p. 210)

Let's consider how survivor siblings describe their experience in treatment as patients, in an effort to illuminate conditions that facilitate (and prevent) the emergence of mediated unexperienced-experience within the therapeutic setting.

References

Atlas, G., & Aron, L. (2018). *Dramatic dialogue: Contemporary clinical practice.* Routledge.

Barnett, M. (2007). What brings you here? An exploration of the unconscious motivations of those who choose to train and work as psychotherapists and counselors. *Psychodynamic Practice: Individuals, Groups and Organizations, 13,* 257–274.

Bollas, C. (1987). *The shadow of the object: Psychoanalysis of the unthought known.* Free Association Books.

Boss, P. (1999). *Ambiguous loss: Learning to live with unresolved grief.* Harvard University Press.

Bowlby, J. (1960). Grief and mourning in infancy and early childhood. *Psychoanalytic Study of the Child, 15,* 9–52.

Caplan, R. (2011). Someone else can use this time more than me: Working with college Students with impaired siblings. *Journal of College Student Psychotherapy, 25,* 120–131.

DeYoung, P. (2015). *Understanding and treating chronic shame: A relational/neurobiological approach.* Routledge.

Farber, S. K. (Ed.). (2017). *Celebrating the wounded healer psychotherapist: Pain, posttraumatic growth and self-disclosure.* Routledge.

Gerson, B. (Ed.). (1996). *Relational perspectives book series, Vol. 6. The therapist as a person: Life crises, life choices, life experiences, and their effects on treatment.* Analytic Press, Inc.

Harris, A. (2009). You must remember this. *Psychoanalytic Dialogues, 19*(1), 2–21.

Hopenwasser, K. (2008). Being in rhythm: Dissociative attunement in therapeutic process. *Journal of Trauma & Dissociation, 9*(3), 349–367.

Klein, M. (1940). Mourning and its relation to manic-depressive states. *International Journal of Psycho-Analysis, 21,* 125–153.

Kuchuck, S. (2014). *Clinical implications of the psychoanalyst's life experience: When the personal becomes professional.* Routledge.

Ogden, P. (1989). *The primitive edge of experience.* Rowman & Littlefield Publishers, Inc.

Perlman, S. (1999). *The therapist's emotional survival: Dealing with the pain of exploring trauma.* Jason Aronson Inc.

Pizer, S. A. (1992). The negotiation of paradox in the analytic process. *Psychoanalytic Dialogues, 2*(2), 215–240.

Safer, J. (2002). *The normal one: Life with a difficult or damaged sibling.* The Free Press.

Schaffer, A. (2006). The analyst's curative fantasies. *Contemporary Psychoanalysis, 42*(3), 349–366.

Stern, D. B. (1983). Unformulated experience: From familiar chaos to creative disorder. *Contemporary Psychoanalysis, 19,* 71–99.

Stern, D. B. (2004). The eye sees itself: Dissociation, enactment, and the achievement of conflict. *Contemporary Psychoanalysis, 40,* 197–237.

Stern, D. B. (2019). *The infinity of the unsaid: Unformulated experience, language and the non-verbal.* Routledge.

Sussman, M. (1992). *A curious calling.* Jason Aronson.

Tessman, L. H. (2003). *The analyst's analyst within.* The Analytic Press.

Winnicott, D. W. (1951). Transitional objects and transitional phenomena. In *Playing & reality* (pp. 1–34). Routledge.

Winnicott, D. W. (1958). The capacity to be alone. In *The maturational process and the facilitating environment: Studies in the theory of emotional development* (pp. 29–36). Karnac.

Winnicott, D. W. (1965). Ego distortions in terms of true and false self. In *The maturational processes and the facilitating environment; studies in the theory of emotional development* (pp. 140–153). Karnac.

Chapter 6

Survivor siblings in treatment

By my senior year of high school things had gotten sufficiently chaotic enough internally for me that I was seeing a therapist. There are a few things I can still recall about this pivotal first experience in treatment. The therapist I was seeing had the uncanny capacity to have me work in parts at a time when it was not yet trendy to do so. This really stands out. My categories for self-experience were not yet as nuanced as they'd later become – in high school I remember calling parts of myself "Good Girl" and "Bad Girl," and feeling that these two parts had nothing to do with one another, except for sharing my body and yet, they both felt like me.

My therapist at the time had me move from one chair to another, encouraging these self states to talk to one another as they spatially felt themselves to be in completely different seats from each other (although without the amnesia that characterizes full blown dissociative identity disorder). I self-consciously complied and, from what I recall, this experiential process resulted in some early reckoning that both parts of myself held a range of complicated, un-expressed feelings about my brother, his condition, and the felt sense of heightened responsibility that went along with not bringing too much of these feelings to my parents. Each self-state had their own characteristic ways of seeking intra-psychic relief from the tension of the family environment that made internal collaboration between them unlikely. The conflict outside was thus relocated inside to an un-ending experience of feeling myself hijacked by two different kinds of drivers, leaving me with a profound sense of confusion about which version of myself to trust, with unevenness, chaos, and shame as the result.

At some point during the treatment, my therapist thought it would be good to invite my mother into a session to discuss this. I cannot for the life of me recall how I went into the appointment, probably an indicator of dissociation, but I do remember some of what happened during and after. I recall sharing that I had been troubled by memories of my brother's seizures and how confused I felt during them when my mom responded with either absence or intensity. That I had some difficultly discerning the reality of the situation because her affect was either turned up too loud or shut off completely, and how we would not as a family process it after he was stabilized again. All of this was conveyed in teenage words, which I can no longer emulate so easily, but as I write now I can feel the uncanniness of the double quality my disclosure evoked in me. The sense that it was absolutely true, while also unreal, or someone else's story. My mom swiftly responded with "I did the best I could," followed by non-stop tears. Nothing broke her, but it appeared that my words just had. Her sense of shame and sorrow filled the room, and it spilled over into me, leaving me feeling certain I had done something really wrong. I imagined it was her shame, not sadness for me, that came out in response to my disclosure of what now felt surely treasonous to have said. I looked to the therapist to help right this dialogue and remedy my mom's injury, but she was not able to make my mom ready for such a talk or to offer me any protection from my mom's woundedness.

A wave of rage washed over me when I realized that the therapist could not protect me from this and had, unwittingly, destroyed Good Girl's primary agenda of not bringing my mother any further pain. My mom walked out of that session and did not speak to me for a few days. So thick and complete was her disturbance that she cut me out – something my verbally enchanted mother had never done before. We never worked through what happened there – neither me and my mom nor me and the therapist. I carried it with me to every therapy afterwards, quite sure that if I unleashed the fullness of my own feelings it would injure those I loved and needed the most, and it would come at the expense of my own emotional safety.

Inhabitation, healing, and the right environment

It was not until my training analysis that I finally had an experience of beginning to integrate the impact of my being a survivor sibling on my life and fragmented/segmented sense of self in a mutative manner. In the interim during and after college, I'd exhausted any hope of getting relief from a one-person treatment. While I found these prior attempts sought with ego-psychologically oriented analysts illuminating in other ways, the last thing I felt I needed was to be left alone with an interpreter of my psyche.[1] I can still recall the strange and frightening somatic experiences I'd have on the couch of being cut off at the knees, or times where my ordinarily busy mind would go completely blank leaving me without *any* language to express the experience of shut-off-ness. When I'd recover speech well enough to share these somatic experiences with these more classically oriented analysts, it never seemed to bring us into the relational land of my wheelchair bound non-verbal brother or our family life. Instead, it was often interpreted to me as my own resistance to being analyzed or, more humiliatingly, as my enactive wish for parental attention, which left me feeling both at fault and foggy about what actually ailed me. I am sure my own dissociative process made this experience hard to translate and represent clinically, but I also think the ego-psychologically driven analytic stance contributed to obfuscating any genuine consideration of the lateral dimension of my particular experience as a survivor sibling. Ego-oriented analytic work, as well as self-psychological and object relational orientations, assume the presence of an underlying unitary self. For me, the difficulty was not between conscious and unconscious experience, but instead between varying self-states, all of which had vast regions of dissociated content waiting to be(come) encountered. The developmental model did not fit.

By the time I found my way to a Relational treatment, it felt long overdue. I still hold onto the words my training analyst gave me, which finally conveyed a sense of being understood. She described my environment as traumatic and over-stimulating *to me*. This of course was not relegated only to my disabled brother and his condition but encompassed something of what it was like to grow up around an unrelenting too muchness, of which his condition and our familial fragility was a big part. This trauma-informed developmental perspective was instrumental in the creation of a therapeutic environment that could engage the dimension of unexperienced-experience therapeutically.

Aside from a book by Tessman (2003) and one forthcoming by Kuchuck (in press), very little explicit research has been done on the relationship an analyst has to their analyst intrapsychically. It is well understood that to become an analyst, one has to go through one's own analysis.

The ideas, attitudes, stances, and affective presence of being with one's analyst shapes the analyst we eventually become. In Tessman's (2003) study, what distinguished deeply satisfying analytic encounters from less fulfilling encounters included basic attitudes toward the patient, helpful ways of communicating, and the quality of the affective presence of the analyst. This chapter considers not only survivor siblings' experience in treatment but also how they internalize their analyst's understanding (or misunderstandings) of their sibling experience. Because the sibling relationship in general is under-theorized, but also because cases of severely disabled siblings are not well represented, many analyses do not get to this material as a lived dyadic experience between them in the clinical moment. An unmentalized experience is very difficult to represent in treatment without an analyst open to understanding how it may be reenacted, and consequently, may leave a survivor sibling without language to name what it is they survived. Davies and Frawley (1994) write:

> Such reenactments involve the unconscious recreation in the treatment setting of dissociatively unavailable aspects of self and object representation – aspects that cannot be verbally described but can via projective-introjective mechanisms, particularly projective-identification volley back and forth between patient and therapist in startling reconstructions of early trauma. . . . Within this model, re-enactments are crucial.
>
> (p. 3)

A repetition of early family life where the issue remains unmentalized or, when present, referenced concretely, is apt to get replayed in the treatment situation (Fonagy et al., 2002). What constitutes a breakthrough in these conditions? What is it about certain analyses that help survivor siblings get affectively in touch with the impact of their experience within the sibling dimension? How might analysts be more equipped to hold in mind these abling/disabling transferences along the lateral dimension while in process? What qualities in the survivor and in the analyst may be most conducive to facilitate this? This chapter aims at answering these questions through the stories told by survivor siblings about the analyses they had, the ones they wished they had, and the ones they might be having now.

Making room for the multiplicity of experience with regard to survivorship

The stunning thing that happened in my first treatment is how quickly and unceremoniously I felt the therapist drop Good Girl. When I think back now, I imagine she must have been concerned with the secretive behavior Bad Girl was up to and that she thought she could reel Bad Girl in by offering her some help for the guilty and confused feelings she harbored inside, which seemingly motivated such self-recklessness. I imagine she reasoned that if my mom could validate those feelings, the self-neglecting errands would come to feel less compelling. Unfortunately by making these assumptions, she left Good Girl behind and elevated Bad Girl to the role of patient with a capitol "P." What had once felt like a space in which different self-states were welcomed and carefully attended to had not so subtlety become a reform school for Bad Girl. Good Girl existed for a reason; compliance is never any kid's first choice. Good Girl then felt betrayed, her only conclusion that the therapist did not care about her or her safety. While the therapist likely felt she was looking out for my well-being, aligning with only a part of the self-system creates therapeutic impasses that require attention, particularly when you involve actual figures of attachment in the treatment.

I think it is very hard to make room for the multiplicity of self for those analysts who did not grow up in a Relational environment. Even for those colleagues who do and have trained within a Relational environment, there can be great difficultly integrating and centering the multiplicity of self into one's work/way of being. The notion that a unified self is an adaptive illusion not to be taken for granted is not so easily placed at the center of one's working model (Bromberg, 1998). Unless it makes intuitive sense and links up with one's own subjective experience, it may not come so naturally to work this way. My intention here is not to pass judgment on different ways of working but to inspire the current generation of analysts with the crucial importance of grasping and working with multiplicity in treating trauma survivors of all kinds.

Not all Relationalists can or choose to think of the self as multiple, but trauma research and neuroscience have gone a long way in informing psychoanalysis. Both disciplines demonstrate how survivorship entails a

splitting of the self and congruent object representations into various identifications that go along with surviving, and that these selves are stored in
the right brain, meaning that they are not initially available linguistically
for translation (Schore, 1994). It follows that for an analysis to awaken
unexperienced-experience, it must be assumed that more than one "I"
(self-state) will need to attend treatment concurrently – who may or may
not have a waking-relationship to one another – and will call forth different I's within the analyst (Davies & Frawley, 1994). In practice, this can be
a deeply creative and unsettling experience. The therapeutic relationship
itself becomes the vehicle in which these self/other representations take
shape and are transformed. The analyst uses their psychobiological attunement to the patient's multiplicity to create an environment in which affect-
regulation is provided, allowing self-state awareness to develop without
shame shutting the process down prematurely (Schore, 2005). This modi-
fies the underlying dissociative structure, in addition to making unconscious experience accessible.

There are many clinical approaches that include multiplicity as a cornerstone of clinical work, such as Internal Family Systems, parts-based work
in Gestalt therapy, and most trauma-informed approaches. Both psychoanalysis, Davies and Frawley (1994), Bromberg (1994, 1998, 2003), D. B.
Stern (2002, 2003, 2004) and those who write about treating severe dissociative disorders analytically, all construct models of therapeutic action
around a baseline appreciation for the multiplicity of self (Chefetz, 2015;
Howell, 2011; Howell & Itzkowitz, 2016; Kluft, 2013; Putnam, 2016).

Partialized help and the problem of unitary-self bias

Even though some writers eloquently represent this clinical perspective,
I suspect that working this way is not as common as the literature would
have us believe. In fact, many of the interviewees conveyed a sense of
having received what I consider *partialized* help in their treatments. Partialized help is defined by a particular self-state receiving care as if they
represented the total sum of the person or the patient's "truest" self. I think
of this as help for one of the "I's." Treatments that assume a unitary self-
structure often go along working within the survivor's non-dissociated
self-state(s) and take for granted that a continuity of self exists, when in
fact, there are dissociative barriers. It may really help to have this resonance and relatedness between these permissible/familiar self-states and

the analyst. And yet, structural change is more apt to occur if the analyst operates from a place of multiplicity, which fosters relatedness between various self-states rather than utilizing a topographical theory of mind, which presumes continuity in self-experience even if a singular unconscious remains clouded in mystery.

For example, instead of treating a depressive expression as a mood/state attributable to the entirety of the self, working from a place of multiplicity might treat the expressive symptom as the emergence of another part of a patient's experience that holds, say, hopelessness, which may or may not have a direct link to other states of mind. If this event occurred in a treatment assuming a unitary self, you might be inclined to think that the depression is the unconscious breaking through and its meaning should be made conscious to unburden the true self underneath. But you'd miss a chance to approach it from a place of multiplicity, where you enlist the patient in identifying what function this self-state is serving and why, deepening a subjectivity that may be evaded in the day to day, by forming a relationship to it. You may also be apt to (mis)interpret the symptom as conveying a transferential communication to you, the object, as opposed to an intra-internal message given by one dissociated self-state to the rest of the self-system *through* you, the analyst, as translator. Of course, the communication can be both intra- and interpersonally driven. But the underlying assumption about the unitary or multiplicity of self affects how the analyst hears and responds to these communications. These are nuanced differences so subtle it might not seem like they are that far apart, but the underlying assumptions about the model of self have impactful consequences.

With trauma survivors, the division is within the self rather than between what is conscious and what remains unconscious in one-self. Unconscious experience permeates the whole self-system and is not located in opposition to either a person's defenses or their unitary conscious self. If compliance belies an attachment to an object that requires submission, that part of the self (experience) is in no way less relevant or less real than the part of the self that is "true" or yearning for emancipation from the felt necessity of submission that the attachment system requires (Ghent, 1990; Winnicott, 1960). Working with multiplicity approaches what we usually think of as defenses as self-states instead, which are not barriers to self-awareness, but actual fragments and representations of self-experience. Rather than something to be overcome, dissociated enactive self-states are badly in need of a relationship to another to be translated. To reduce a shift in self-state to a change in mood is to misunderstand that whole worldviews and varying capacities are contained within self-states. Entering into a different self-state can affect the way you feel, look, sense, and see what happened in the past and what's happening around you now. Without repair to the underlying dissociative structure, a positive change in a self-state will not necessarily translate across the inter-systemic self-system. And while it may be tempting to align with the self-state that seems healthiest and treat it as the "real" one, an analyst that mistakes a part for the whole will miss a chance to repair the underlying dissociative structure, reinforcing a reliance on the dissociative process.

Survivor siblings themselves identify with pleasing self-states and struggle to discard and dissociate less tolerable ones. The underlying dissociative structure will be very disabling in a treatment that assumes a unitary self. To give you a sense of what I mean, here are some comments from survivor siblings who felt they received partialized benefit from analysis.

Marisa, the most senior in degree of clinical experience within the sample, recalled her first analysis during her adolescence with fondness and idealization. When asked for examples of what led to this glowing recollection, she said her analyst interpreted that she'd "*denied her sister's existence in an attempt to gain retribution*" for her feelings of being unattended to by her parents. **Marisa** felt this was "*interesting,*" meaning it reached her cerebrally, but not affectively, as it did not seem to fundamentally change her inner relationship to her own survivorship. She relayed that she subjectively felt herself as "*invaded, scarred, and defective.*" This early treatment helped her orient to a part of her experience. "*It was like a class of what's going on inside of me as my analyst immediately saw I had murderous rage towards my sister. My head was exploding. It felt like an enlightenment to acknowledge these feelings.*" She tells me how much she idealized this treatment and actually links it with her becoming an analyst herself. Looking back, she sees how her analyst leaned into Anna Freud and her concepts of ego defenses in understanding what **Marisa** did in order to survive an environment that was "*100% focused*" on her disabled sister's care. I was not at all prepared for what came next, as she casually told me, "*In the end my analyst kicked me out of treatment, because I could not express my aggression toward her. I think she got frustrated.*"

The best way I can make sense of what might have happened here is that the analyst felt **Marisa's** aggression toward the self and the sister needed to be turned toward the mother/analyst for her to be liberated. An ego-psychologically driven approach is going to conceptualize **Marisa's** experience along conscious and unconscious lines and treat the unconscious content as primary. What might have happened if she had been given room to represent the parts of her that feared and could not use aggression turned outwards? Rather than viewing this as hostile, resistant, or hopeless, what could have emerged if this part of **Marisa** was engaged with rather than analyzed out of the treatment? How might this analyst have used the induced frustration to translate and enliven a dissociated self-state of **Marisa's**?

In another instance, the topic of siblings itself was off limits, perhaps in part due to the analyst's own dissociated relationship to disability:

Carolyn: It still amazes me that my sibling experience was never a serious topic of my work in a ten year long treatment. Oddly my analyst had a son who had a learning disability, and I never put that together either until now. Initially I sought treatment when I was first pregnant and fearing something would go wrong, and the analysis focused on my conflicts around motherhood.

This enterprise evaded entirely her complicated survivorship history and missed the opportunity to link her fears of motherhood to the caretaking legacy of her disabled sibling, for whom she functioned as a primary attachment figure. As we talked together, it became more and more apparent how the treatment was for the parts of self that were not connected to her survivorship. The fantasized unharmed or free self, who had anxieties located in other realms of existence, participated in the treatment, while the parts of her that were linked to survival remained imaginatively located back in the past. What happened between them that the realm of survivorship remained unacknowledged? How might her fears with caretaking have led them back to her direct experience of caretaking for her sister and parents and the parts of herself that held these memories?

In the next two examples, the analytic space could not hold or engage those self-states associated with the sensory-overload of being a survivor sibling, though they could see and treat the more familiar aspect of grief:

Susan: My analyst totally did not get internal dynamics around care in my family. They could not go through or conceive of it, so I didn't even try to explain. But what my analyst did get was the grieving and mourning it required. Since my sister ultimately died, my analyst helped me to realize I had never done the work of mourning, and conveyed the sense of a sister is a sister is a sister

Again, we can hear how helpful it was for **Susan** to gain an opportunity to mourn her sister's passing. But other aspects of her survivorship go unrepresented and un-mourned. What about self-states of **Susan** that held the feelings around caretaking for her sister when she was living? Or the parts of her that did not feel, say, only grief about her passing? Or the parts of her that continued to operate in her present tense that were/are deeply impacted by her sister's condition?

Natalie also receives help from the analysis in mourning the death of her sister, but the space for holding contradiction does not appear present:

Natalie: Fortunately when I did my first analysis, my psychoanalyst was a very old woman, who had a lot of sensitivity and empathy and this allowed me to understand that my sister was not only different, but in spite of her illness she could give me the best life lesson. This does not mean that it was easy; it was very painful for me to accept that I was normal and she was not, that I could do what I expected from a life and she did not, and above all it was very painful to accept her death. I think it was more painful for me to accept this death than this illness.

She is taking away a lesson from the analyst that may be serving the emotional needs of a part of herself and the analyst, but we should not assume speaks for the entirety of the self.

Even under more resonant conditions where the analyst engaged the multiplicity of self, sometimes enactments between analyst and patient stopped at the entry point of repetition. Rather than becoming portals into a widened felt sense of self-state integration, an alliance with a part was formed inadvertently excluding other self-states:

Olina: *The first treatment helped me to realize how many feelings I had warded off and how fearful I was to encounter negative feelings, especially feeling them in my body. In the next treatment, my analyst shared having had a "damaged sibling" purposely, and I still recall feeling so split about that word. Part of me loved hearing it named plainly but another part of me felt that it was wrong to*

> *say. So much political correctness, and then I was left wondering,
> where do I get support for the damaged me?*

Olina did not feel able to articulate these later feelings regarding the analyst's disclosure, and this ripe enactment became stale as she accommodated her analyst's need to identify with her wellness rather than unpack
the multiplicity of her own identifications. This also repeats the lopsided
caregiving dimension described in Chapter 4.

Other times, the analytic focus on the sibling actually missed engaging
the representation of the damaged self. In other words, the dissociated
damaged self-state is treated as if it does not reside within the patient.
Kira states, *"I was a year into treatment when my sister ultimately died,
while I was pregnant with my first child."* **Kira** knew from ultrasounds
that her first child had a very mild deformity and her therapist kept explicitly linking her experience of mothering a mildly disabled baby with her
experience of being her sister's sister. **Kira** felt this was especially unem-
pathic, as her sister's condition was entirely debilitating and her son's
was far less restrictive; it felt to her like a categorical difference entirely.
Kira tells me of a dream she had in this treatment, where she is rushing
to get to the floor of the hospital where her sister is (which is also where
she works), to take care of her, but when she finally arrives, she discovers
her sister is well cared for and does not need her. From the vantage point
of a self-state dream, the content felt representative of her own psychic
structure and how well she buried the one who is ill in wellness, right
before their eyes.

To be clear, I think that analysts' lack of attention to or elaboration
of the lateral dimension, awareness of particularities of living among
chronic illness as a variable (as opposed to the more familiar territory of early death/separation), as well as patients' own need to keep
at bay dissociated self-states that are felt as both internally and externally destabilizing, all converge to create a fortress that reinforces
the shield around unexperienced-experience as opposed to unearthing
it. How might these analysts and survivor siblings have gotten to the
unexperienced-experience held within the dissociated self-states? The
framework of the analyst adopting a parts-based approach to the work
and looking for the subtle shifts in self-state, makes room for all parts of
the patient in the treatment by attending to their own discordant counter-transferential reactions – to cross the bridge of dissociation is to
make use of enactment.

Engaging dissociative multiplicity through the vehicle of re/enactments

Stern (1983, 2019) writes prolifically on the inevitability of enactments when working with dissociated, or as he calls it, unformulated experience. Because it does not yet exist to be found, it can only be brought into the space through (self-state) action, and this action can include inaction. Enactments to me are the repetition compulsion in an interactive matrix, which includes the presence of the analyst's subjectivity and involvement. Instead of thinking a patient is bringing the "then and there" to the here and now, enactments are opportunities to experience how here and now between us is experientially revived and connected to where the "You's" were, then and there. Close scrutiny of one's own internal experience in sitting with a patient is an essential part of monitoring the process of dissociative content and the unformulated realm. A change in internal state, focus, perception, mood, or feeling is often the first indicator of the presence of such dissociated content and an analyst who can respectfully, but tactfully name these states (definitely internally and sometimes externally), does a great service in making use of the unconscious communication (Bromberg, 1994). Bromberg writes:

> Before these "not-me" states of mind can be taken as objects of analytic self-reflection, they must first become "thinkable"; while becoming linguistically communicable through enactment in the analytic relationship. This depends on the analyst's ability to acknowledge the divergent realities held by discontinuous self-states in the patient while simultaneously maintaining an authentic dialogue with each. By "unfreezing" the concrete, literal quality of a patient's discontinuous states of consciousness, the patient is able to embrace the full range of his perceptual reality within a single relational field, so that the process becomes a dialectic between seeing and being seen rather than simply being seen "into."
>
> (p. 517)

Many times, the dissociated content is experienced as a kind of relational projective identification whereby the analyst feels it belong to themselves plus *something more*. The something more becomes the unnamed/unmarked communication to attend to. This necessitates a tolerance for not-knowing what the *something more* means or is or how it might be understood, and for being forgiving towards oneself for not knowing. Shame I think interferes so much for both patient and analyst alike in tolerating dissociated communications. Listen to John Sloane's (2017) voice, an analyst in his seventies as he writes in his chapter on being a wounded healer:

> I am often unable to understand or alleviate the pain, torn by conflicts I cannot resolve, ashamed of my temporary but timeless ignorance and impotence, and saddened by grief that does not go away. Strangely though I have learned that by bearing such pain, powerlessness, shame, rage and despair without taking refuge in premature knowing and doing, healing happens.
>
> (p. 201)

These are the portals into unexperienced-experience but they are laden with pitfalls that make bearing vulnerability with affective presence alive on both sides very hard. Just think about it: An experience too painful to have inhabited in real-time means both patient and analyst will likely encounter being and experiencing themselves as really gruesome. If this were not the case, the experience would not have needed to be dissociated in the first place.

As a wounded healer who comes to the profession at least in part for their own relief, it is not easy to hold shame-ridden, disgust-filled, anger-fueled hopelessness, especially because, as it happens, in the process you do not initially have an outside perspective on what it is that's being inhabited. In fact, the struggle to regain the third, or a way of both looking while inhabiting the encounter, is the skill of the analyst, and one that over time also hopefully transfers to the patient (Benjamin, 2004). In the meantime, you have to hold such states as looking and feeling incompetent, useless, worthless, phony, not good enough, not able to help, or some other difficult position of complementarity vis-à-vis the patient, all of which is painfully difficult. The survivor sibling may hold in turn the complementary states of feeling that they are truly beyond help, responsible for even the incompetent analyst toward whom they may not even be able to voice such aggression, never mind longing, unable to be seen, unable to be soothed, unable to be free of this legacy, or to feel they occupy it any differently than the traumatic ways of the past.

Entering into unexperienced-experience can get very bleak, very fast. It reminds me of Rick Kluft's (2013) adage that the slower you go, the faster you get there, and the way he carefully considers time and volume in the pacing of therapeutic processing. Titrating exposure to match a patient's evolving capacities also ensures the analyst can maintain affective presence, two necessary relational conditions for the inhabitation of experience. Because you need to be able to build up tolerance to occupy such experiences in a way that will facilitate inhabitation as opposed to activating further fragmentation, the specialized skills and knowledge of the analyst really matter here (Kluft, 2013). The examples that follow include some illustrations of analysts making use of the enactments between them and the survivor sibling patient, in ways that imply the possession of such therapeutic skills. You'll notice that in these instances, the analyst is able to implicitly make room for that which has yet to appear/come into being.

Hannah: My first analyst had been Freudian, and was not very clued into me. I remember he would mis-identify people in my life. I didn't say much then. The second analyst I saw came from an interpersonal training and understood something about schizoid phenomena. He really helped me plug into being a person. I remember he noticed the ways in which I was "not there."

Hannah linked this memory up to an experience she had as a child of becoming very adept at not needing. She went on to relay,

> *But then I was sitting there in treatment and he understood something about that. I somehow found an analyst who had things "for me," and for the first time, it opened up the possibility of realizing what I'd gone without.*

Darlene: In my third treatment my analyst brought her dog to session. It was a small, needy, non-verbal presence, and I felt an acute interruption, like something else was occupying a part of her mind, like some part of her mind was always elsewhere. Because she was so skilled and sensitive, my reaction to the dog led us to my sister. A parallel part of me felt, "get the dog out of here," while another part was ravaged by guilt for wanting all of her attention too. She really recognized something meaningful going on in this for me, and repeatedly brought it up, when I might have skipped over it. The one thing analysis has offered me is the recognition that my sister will always be a traumatic loss to me, however, I shift into a position where I actually feel a deeper connection to her, in bearing this recognition.

For **Selena**, her brother's genetic condition ultimately robbed him of life earlier than the other stories included in my sample, and as she discussed her four treatments, different themes came to light. **Selena** lived her survivorship in a powerfully damaging way by believing that it was her own anger that contributed to her brother's death. She recalled kicking him too hard while playing together in the days leading up to his untimely end. She had told no one about the kicking, and so when he died it left her feeling her anger was capable of killing others. This self-state pervaded her entire sense of self. It was not until her fourth analysis that she could "*talk about my anger toward my brother, and my parents about how they handled everything.*" This analyst helped her to "*understand my mother without being too identified with her,*" and gave her room to use "*my anger in a creative way, in being an analyst who can feel things.*" The earlier treatments reenacted the guilty positionality of her murderous self-state without linking it to her lived experience rendering the material not yet inhabitable.

Debra: In my first psychotherapy, the therapist occupied the shared lacuna I was in about this un-imagined space where my feelings for my sister resided. It was frozen, unchangeable, and inaccessible. But once I began a four times a week analysis for training, I was stunned that my analyst kept hearing references to my sister, which I did not hear. It was hugely relieving to me that he could hear this, all these unconscious phantasies of what could happen to me because of what had happened to her – it was just life altering. Siblings are the dirty little secret of psychoanalysis, somehow we get handed down from Freud the importance of parents, but not siblings. My analyst does siblings.

I learned of another enactment while I was interviewing **Claire**, who in the course of our interview revealed to me that it was her analyst who notified her of my study. The other participants saw my query directly, but in this case, Claire's analyst saw it, thought of her, and shared it with her. What might this communication have conveyed to Claire in terms of an interpretation-through-action? Or what might have been enacted between them through the analyst's suggestion that she look into the study? While I do not know for sure, I like to think that the analyst was inviting Claire to more fully inhabit her lived experience. Claire seemingly made great use of this enactment by contacting me and participating in the study unearthing her own realm of unexperienced-experienced throughout our dialogue. I like to imagine this opened up areas for experiencing between her and the analyst too, and that her analyst's suggesting she learn more was felt as an invitation to Claire's dissociated self-states about inhabiting their survivorship experiences more directly in the treatment.

The stories of treatments that broke new ground and reached dissociated content seemed to be had by analysts who were consistently and empathically skeptical of the unilateral presentation of over-abledness in their patients with survivor histories and who could consider and allow for a multitude of transferential/countertransferential relivings to unfold, sometimes all at the same time. Frequently, common content that became encountered counter-transferentially in enactments involved analysts being cast in the role of either disabled sibling, unknowing parent, or the absent active patient self – all self-states connected to **unexperienced-experience**. Here are some illustrations of treatments that illuminate the countertransferential position of dissociated self/object relations:

Absent active self:

Harold: In my second analysis, the central place of my brother in my psychic life is much more alive, like embers in a fireplace. I thought I already had water splashed on them but this analysis is bringing it to life between us. I describe it like having a much more Windexed window into my own childhood experience. Overall it allows me to come to terms with being dissociative, recognizing that there are feelings there that I am not sufficiently connected to. My analyst is challenging me more to identify where I am in the stories I tell, and showing me how I narrate myself through absence.

Unknowing parent/disabled sibling:

Rose: I was 10 years into analytic treatment, and I was hating my analyst. I thought repeatedly, "This isn't working, I'm still fucked up." My analyst then made an unconventional call to have me consult with a colleague and I'll never forget what he said to me when I described what was happening in the treatment. He said "It seems you want to discard yourself and I think that's about your sister." This changed everything – it opened the door to my realizing how angry I was at my analyst for not helping me work on these issues. Once this experience became "front and center" everything changed. Up to that point, no one had confronted me on the fantasy I harbored of my anger having gotten rid of her, and I was desperate for someone to see the stakes. We enacted it, by my wanting to be rid of the analyst, but my analyst was wise enough to have me consult with a third party who could see what was getting played out between us. She went from unhelpful to extremely helpful.

Unknowing parent/disabled sibling:

Rachel: My training analysis did not cover my experience of my sister and with my family. I don't know why entirely but I am sure I am culpable for it. This is much more alive in my treatment now. There is a lot of resistance – analysts really lack the words to talk about this kind of thing. My current analyst though, she really knows me, she doesn't rush in to criticize anyone, has a "there's no one to blame here" approach, which lets me access my shame. She does a really good job of making me look at the story beneath the story. I idealized my mother so much that I have selectively not paid attention to the ways in which she really was un-available to me, and so my analyst calls my attention to the ways in which I too easily let people off the hook, including her. We also attend to the bad feelings generated in me around my disabled sister. My sister is taxing, intrusive, disruptive, it's not a quiet existence. Having the space to acknowledge the frustration, shame, aggression, anger, even my disgust, makes a big difference in how I live with it.

In each of these brief examples, dissociated content gets enacted in the transferential/countertransferential domain, but it is the mentalizing capacity of the analyst and patient together that makes the experience generative as opposed to just repetitive (Atlas & Aron, 2018; Bromberg, 1994, 1998). For survivor siblings, enactments make the unexperienced-experience of survivorship – both its impact on the self system and its objects – near and accessible in the clinical moment for formulation. It cannot be thought first, it is not encoded verbally. It is brought into the room through the affective environment created by the patient's and analyst's varying self-states. Repetition becomes a generative enactment when an analyst is able to receive and relate to each self-state of the patient. The fragmentation of selfhood wrought by survivorship is painstakingly made bearable and reworked as these fragmentations become embodied and in-relationship to other parts of the self, and the analyst. One way to think about a generative enactment is that it establishes a conscious connection to a self-state, previously left out of experiential life and treatment, that is now with the person, and in the room, for better and for worse. This process is as true for the analyst as it is for the patient, as Jody Davies (2004) rightly shows us in her welcoming one of her own "bad" self-states over the course of treatment with a patient, for whom this part of Jody's participation was necessary for her own healing. Going further still, Benatar (2004) writes:

> Much attention has been given to the negative effects of intense long-term work with trauma survivors. However, recognition of secondary traumatization effects does not exclude the possibility of what I am call-ing positive self transformation – the more salubrious effects of being a trauma therapist. Therapists who are able to successfully rework and adapt within themselves will be able to transform re-enactments and not merely repeat with the patient unconscious failures.
>
> (p. 13)

Conclusion

How can an analyst engage the multiplicity of self-regarding sibling survivorship in the treatment room? For me, it involves making contact with the self-state that is present and holding that contact, but not exclusively, even if it is only in your awareness as an analyst of there being other inner selves who might want or need something very different from what is being pursued or understood or considered in this moment. You treat the patient as a team, and you foster a relationship with each of their play-ers, whether they know about them or not, whether they identify or disi-dentify with them or not. You implicitly make room for what has not yet become formulated. Survivor siblings can grow into the spaces they have vacated more easily if they sense there is room for them to do so in the experiencing mind and body of their analyst. If developmental trauma is an assault on the capacity to integrate the experience into a coherent and fluid self-system, the framework for treatment involves creating the environmental conditions that bring disparate parts of unexperienced-experience together (Siegel, 1999). This implies an experiential process, not an insight-knowledge driven one. The mechanism by which this happens is born out through the relational space and unconscious enactive communications within and between analyst and patient (Bromberg, 1998). An analyst who can "house" internally a survivor's *not-me* self-states brings uninhabited experience gradually into the relational field for reabsorption and conscious reflection.

In clinical practice, survivors often have their not-me self-states begin within the analyst through the counter-transferential experience before inhabiting them as their own. If you treat the projective process of patients as about exclusively or primarily their objects, you may miss a chance to align and develop a relationship to a dissociated self-state that's operative in you, the analyst. Are you bored? Maybe feeling helpless? Too constrained or bogged down by the demands of reality? Not sure what role there is to play in the patient's life because their competency crowds you out? Irritated that there is no vulnerability here? Or that it shows up as a closed system of self-attack? These are all opportunities to occupy what may have been vacated in the survivor sibling, to speak from *inside that place*, and by doing so, gently hand back a self-state that has been unattached, floating off in the dissociative waters around its host. Gradually, bit by bit, once you facilitate inhabitation in this way, you make sure to keep creating room for other parts of experience, such as self-states tied to competency or loyalty to parents or longing for the missing sibling other, or any of the specific configurations that result in making the subjectivity of a survivor *who they are*. These regions will be different for everyone, but the task of occupying this dizzying multiplicity together and bringing them to life through the reveries held within the mind and body of the shared relational experience is the same across treatments.

As Atlas and Aron (2018) suggest, "Enactments, and not only their interpretation or resolution, are thus a creative medium for giving psychological birth to or actualizing the self" (p. 18). I would just pluralize that to say "selves." Re/enactments offer opportunities to reclaim dissociated self-states, to inhabit unexperienced-experience from the vantage point of presence, which may lend itself to a subjective cohesiveness that was initially absent in development. Survivor siblings who are fortunate enough to have this experience in treatment are better positioned to provide it to others, as they internalize this kind of therapeutic action in vivo themselves. Let's turn to see how survivorship impacts the clinical encounter from opposite the couch.

Note

1 I realize this is just my experience of non-Relational treatments, and that for others, the space to wander in their own psyche without participation/intrusion is a welcomed relief. But given the difficulties I had in encountering *mutually validated experience*, one-person settings for me tended to heighten my own fragmentation without offering any sense of connection or relief. Instead of becoming a subject, I'd feel further alien-like and objectified by the process. I desperately needed a participating other to bring me into contact with the unexperienced–experience.

References

Atlas, G., & Aron, L. (2018). *Dramatic dialogue: Contemporary clinical practice.* Routledge.

Benatar, M. (2004). Purification and the self-system of the therapist. *Trauma & Dissociation, 5*(4), 1–15.

Benjamin, J. (2004). Beyond doer and done to: An intersubjective view of thirdness. *Psychoanalytic Quarterly, 73*, 5–46.

Bromberg, P. M. (1994). Speak! That I may see you: Some reflections on dissociation, reality & psychoanalytic listening. *Psychoanalytic Dialogues, 4*(4), 517–547.

Bromberg, P. M. (1998). *Standing in the spaces: Essays on clinical process, trauma, and dissociation.* The Analytic Press.

Bromberg, P. M. (2003). One need not be a house to be haunted: On enactment, dissociation, and the dread of "not-me": A case study. *Psychoanalytic Dialogues, 13*, 689–709.

Chefetz, R. A. (2015). *Intensive Psychotherapy for persistent dissociative processes: The fear of feeling real.* W.W. Norton.

Davies, J. M. (2004). Whose bad objects are we anyway? Repetition and our elusive love affair with evil. *Psychoanalytic Dialogues, 14*(6), 711–732.

Davies, J. M., & Frawley, M. G. (1994). The impact of trauma on transference/counter-transference. In *Treating the adult survivor of childhood sexual abuse: A psychoanalytic perspective* (pp. 149–166). Basic Books.

Fonagy, P., Gergely, G., Jurist, E., & Target, M. (2002). *Affect regulation, mentalization and the development of the self.* Other Press.

Ghent, E. (1990). Masochism, submission, surrender: Masochism as a perversion of surrender. *Contemporary Psychoanalysis, 26*, 108–136.

Howell, E. F. (2011) *Understanding and Treating Dissociative Identitiy Disorder: A Relationship Approach.* Routledge.

Howell, E., & Itzkowitz, S. (Eds.). (2016). *The dissociative mind in psychoanalysis: Understanding and working with trauma.* Routledge.

Kluft, R. (2013). *Shelter from the storm: Processing the traumatic memories of DID/DDNOS patients with the fractionated abreaction technique.* Create Space Independent Publishing.

Kuchuck, S. (Ed.). (in press). *When the psychoanalyst is the patient.* Routledge.

Putnam, F. (2016). *The way we are: How states of mind influence our identities, personality and potential for change.* International Psychoanalytic Books.

Schore, A. N. (1994). *Affect regulation and the origin of the self.* Routledge.

Schore, A. N. (2005). A neuropsychoanalytic viewpoint. Commentary on paper by Steven H. Knoblauch. *Psychoanalytic Dialogues, 15,* 829–854.

Siegel, D. (1999). *The developing mind: How relationships and the brain interact to shape who we are.* Guilford Press.

Sloane, J. A. (2017). Wounded healer, healing wounder: A personal story. In S. Farber (Ed.), *Celebrating the wounded healer psychotherapist: Pain, post-traumatic growth and self-disclosure* (pp. 201–207). Routledge.

Stern, D. B. (1983). Unformulated experience: From familiar chaos to creative disorder. *Contemporary Psychoanalysis, 19,* 71–99.

Stern, D. B. (2002). Words and wordlessness in the psychoanalytic situation. *Journal of the American Psychoanalytic Association, 50,* 221–247.

Stern, D. B. (2003). The fusion of horizons: Dissociation, enactment, and understanding. *Psychoanalytic Dialogues, 13,* 843–873.

Stern, D. B. (2004). The eye sees itself: Dissociation, enactment, and the achievement of conflict. *Contemporary Psychoanalysis, 40,* 197–237.

Stern, D. B. (2019). *The infinity of the unsaid: Unformulated experience, language and the non-verbal.* Routledge.

Tessman, L. H. (2003). *The analyst's analyst within.* The Analytic Press.

Winnicott, D. W. (1960). Ego distortion in terms of true and false self. In *The maturational process and the facilitating environment: Studies in the theory of emotional development* (pp. 140–152). Karnac.

Chapter 7

Survivor siblings as psychoanalysts

A long-term patient I'd been caring for who lived a profoundly isolating existence prior to and throughout much of the treatment, and who was just forging a capacity to let himself care and be cared for by me within the therapy, came in for a session one day and said,

Patient: I cried again last night. But *(his gaze meeting mine directly)*, don't worry; it wasn't that crying that can't stop. I was watching a YouTube video that was very touching. A girl was taking care of her cat. The cat had cerebral palsy, so it couldn't walk. It might have been in pain, we don't know. But the video shows the girl taking care of this cat, and her family supports this. And it was just so moving.

Me: (Internally marveling that of all things, this cat had CP and realizing I never explicitly told him anything about the relationship between me and CP and that he does not usually notice anything about the impact his distress has on me.)

I hear that. Do you think you were feeling connected to one of the people in the video?

Patient: "Oh, I guess, I don't know. I mean, the thing is, it's the girl taking care of the cat, but she gets something from that too. You can feel that. It was just. . ." *(Trailing off here into feeling, as opposed to out of it for a change.)*

Me: *(Silence.)* So it would be a mistake to say this is a video about what she is giving the cat, because the care goes both ways? It's mutual?

Patient: Yes, that's it! It made her so happy, to be able to have something to give him.

In my head, I'm communing with the straight-shooter Harold Searles (1975) here as he comes readily to mind telling me what a lovely interpretation this patient is giving me. That it is usable for both of us and demonstrative of a new intersubjective space we have now gotten to in the treatment. Searles also tells me that it is ok to enjoy this recognition. In fact, it is necessary as the patient is telling me he knows something about what I derive from giving, and that to be open and honest about that is a part of therapeutic action here. The tentativeness of our togetherness hinges on his recognition that I'm in it too, and that I know and acknowledge the parts of me that gain from having something to give him, just as I struggle when his remoteness disables our connection entirely. That is, my caring for him, and my caring for my brother, give me something too – and this mutuality of caring and being cared for is part of what it means to be a human. That togetherness is possible, despite disability or even because of it. That disability does not preclude connectivity even if it makes it more challenging, for me anyway, to find.

The relationship between wounds, healing, and consciousness

Given the many facets that contribute to becoming an analyst, the multifaceted unconscious derivatives of the survivor sibling psyche are always at play in the context of the work. Even if one recognizes the ways in which being a psychoanalyst both assuages and aggravates the unmirrored early experience of one's disabled/defective selves, there is no limit to how our unconscious experience shapes our participation in the work (Stern, 2019). For Jung, "a good half of every treatment that probes at all deeply consists in the doctor's examining himself . . . it is his own hurt that gives a measure of his power to heal" (Stevens, 1994, p. 110). Jung adopted the term "wounded healer" to capture the phenomena of transmuting the experience of one's own wounds into clinical acumen with patients or, in relational terms, a capacity for embodied presence and witnessing.

Other Relational writers have developed the idea further in capturing the phenomena of analysts who work collaboratively with the ghosts of their, or their ancestors', pasts (Apprey, 2014; Faimberg, 2005; Farber, 2017; Harris, 2009; Harris et al., 2016; Kuchuck, 2014). I call on this metaphor too, in thinking through the complexities of being a survivor sibling analyst. The many wounds surrounding and encompassing unexperienced-experience can become a clinician's greatest teacher – but what conditions facilitate productive encounters from retraumatizing reenactments? Can they even be distinguished? Harris (2009) writes:

> The task of distinguishing clinical responsibility from omnipotence is endless and exacting and always, to some degree, indeterminate. It is never solely the problem of sorting the origins of affect but also bearing the personal affective states, with all their personal historical force, in us.
>
> (p. 9)

Harris asserts that it is the capacity to bear being affectively stirred up and to make use of impasses to rearrange our interior experience that distinguishes productive encounters from reenactments. This creates a third intersubjective space in which something new or something different may happen. What qualities might survivor analysts possess that facilitate and inhibit the capacity to bear experience?

Survivors' clinical capacities

The degree to which the "Achilles Heals" of survivor siblings become gifts to their patients of course depends upon the survivor sibling's inter-systemic self-experience and the degree of awareness regarding the varying levels of motivation driving the work, as discussed in Chapter 5. The more dialectical tensions exist between having/not having, doing/being, and participating/witnessing, the greater the likelihood that survivorship is transmuted into wisdom. Many interviewees elaborated upon such capacities, including an imaginative dwelling to hold silence in the Winnicottian fashion – which is to say that one may still feel deeply connected without assuming silence is the absence of communication or defensiveness (Gabbard, 1989; Khan, 1963; Winnicott, 1958). Interviewees describe a familiarity in being connected to someone nonverbally, which makes the experience of silence less something one has to change, block out, feel reactive toward, or rush to interpret. It is striking how much communication can be imagined in the throes of silence from a patient among survivor sibling analysts. Being able and willing to receive the intended communications held within the silence, without pathologizing the one that is quiet, is a real skill. The complementary experience of holding this silence is the analyst's capacity to communicate nonverbally back to one's patients and to make use of being together and information sharing without words themselves, as in Schlower's concept of holding (Ogden, 1994; Slochower, 1996, 2013) and the neuroscientific notion of psychobiological attunement (Schore, 1994).

Other gifts involve a *willingness* to tolerate and manage extreme affect dysregulation, while maintaining optimal self-awareness of its impact given early, repetitive experiences with it. Survivor siblings often develop a reputation for being good with "difficult patients" for this reason. Whether they actually like being challenged in this way or not is a different matter. And finally, survivor siblings maintain a sharply tuned monitor for loss alongside an empathetic understanding of the defensive maneuvers people use to both cope with and evade it. They can hold, sense, and see what is lost and how the recognition of loss is often evaded, with a gentle, less shaming touch. A reality-based practical knowledge about the limits of growth and the unconscious fantasies it stirs is something none of us lose sight of, as we continually practice coming to terms with it within our personal, familial, and professional life.

But knowing about wounds does not insulate one from either side of the polarity of being wounded or wounding. Sloane (2017) writes, "One way or another, we wind up repeatedly wounding and being wounded on the way toward healing our selves and others" (p. 204). He goes on to explain that the road to healing is never one single destination, so that we may find ourselves being wounded or wounding in *new ways* as we evolve as people and clinicians, so inevitably most of us "never outgrow our need for someone to talk to about where we are coming from, personally" (p. 204). I find this passage exceptionally relieving. To transmute wounds, we need an ongoing meta-dialogue or else we run the risk of what musician Elliott Smith poetically calls "checking into a small reality." Sloane goes on to identify writing as a way to maintain an inner dialogue about our personal experience and evolution, and surely this book is a testament to that. Other mechanisms include treatment, supervision, and peer process groups. To ripen wounds, we must maintain a practice of ongoing presence with our inner selves, something I have come to call meta-dialogue (Dobrich, 2020). This is of course true for all analysts but may be especially heightened for those of us who come to practice with the kinds of embedded wounds tied to identity formation and psychic structure described here.

In this chapter, we'll explore experiences survivor siblings have as clinicians, without trying to artificially catalogue the wounded from the wounding, or the good from the bad. Instead, I'd like to consider how experience always holds all dimensions of any polarity and give a longer listen into the ways in which survivorship may invite a particular kind of listening and presence to the work. This listening is dual, both to the patient, and to the inner selves of the analyst simultaneously, and includes all units of time – past, present, and future – for both parties. The kaleidoscopic shifting in and out of modes of relatedness, and holding the contradictions these various perspectives represent without trying to resolve them or identify with the most pleasing of them, is the hallmark of post-traumatic growth. A genuine, ongoing, inner meta-dialogue is borne of this process that creates the mediated third within a self-system. Resiliency is not borne of resolution, but of tolerating contradiction while sustaining a sense of inner trust. I do not believe this particular listening stance can be taught; it must be acquired through lived experience. It has to cut across the selves and heart to be accessible in a non-cerebral way. You cannot gain resiliency without a sustained encounter of enlivening and inhabiting the unexperienced-experience in which the wounds were first cut. Those selves that got left behind in trauma time are needed in forging a meta-dialogue.

The strange alchemy of turning wounds to wisdom

How do survivor sibling analysts cultivate their faith in the analytic encounter, while managing a felt internal need to make reparation, to lessen the experience gap between the self and the damaged sibling, and to care for the younger often emotionally under-provided for inner-selves? Enriching another's subjectivity always has implications for what we come to know and find in ourselves. Sitting with patients who are suffering can easily collapse here-and-now time into then-and-there for the survivor analyst and invite into the foreground some of the most reactive self-states created to manage the experience of loss. In part, this invitation is the impetus for doing the work, to *feel* these feelings. But it is more than feeling them that we are hoping for. We are hoping for transformation (Bollas, 1979). And so are our patients. How do survivor siblings manage their relationship to growth and its absence in the clinical encounter? In what ways do they use this personal experience of survivorship in their work with patients to facilitate the analytic process without overtaking it and disrupting the asymmetrical but mutual frame (Aron, 1996)?

I believe that treatment, ongoing self-analysis through internal meta-dialogue, and clinical supervision all offer important spaces for alchemizing pain into presence. It is treatment and supervision that help get meta-dialogue back on track when it feels lost. Writing can have a similar effect by sustaining and representing multiple points of view and relatedness (Flax, 2011). For survivors, these experiences are more than learning tools; they are necessary to avoid the repetition of solitary responsibility, which from my vantage point invites some of the less immediately help-ful self-states to the party while rendering others less accessible. If the analyst's self-system is restricted in this way, and the interpersonal field is narrowed often enough, the clinical work gets stuck. As mentioned earlier, this can be a profoundly important place to reach for bringing attention to the presence of the dissociative structures or impossible "object rela-tions" in the transference/countertransference, so by no means should it or can it be avoided; Hopenwasser (2008) explains dissociative attune-ment in just this way. Receiving the unconscious communication requires a loss of conscious connection internally and externally to more fluid ways of being/experiencing. But once this is a felt experience in the room and within the dyad, how to inhabit the enactment and enliven it, implicitly inviting the multiplicity of self and other (back) in, becomes paramount for transformation. Without a fuller house in which a mediatory space arises, the teller of the show-and-tell has no one there to tell. As the selves of the analyst undergo a transformation, and more flexibility is created inter-systemically, so too do the ways in which we work. In addition to managing our own growth, life experience continues to mount, so that for each of us things are in motion:

> Of paramount interest for all clinicians is how the analyst's counter-transference is brought into the treatment situation, how therapists transmit certain values, encouragements, and attitudes to their patients at certain phases of their lives or their development, and how these phenomena may shift and change at another phase.
>
> (Ruderman, 2002, p. 497)

In what follows, I'll describe three thematic pathways in which the self-system of the analyst engages themes of survivorship differently. These are snapshots of a much fuller process and are gleaned from interviewees' reconstruction of past clinical experience, yet certain experiential themes emerged across subjects. These include (1) overestimating one's capacities and experiencing difficulty setting emotional boundaries, (2) maintaining a heightened attunement to loss, and (3) evolving, albeit contradictory, experiences with growth. In each section, we will note the listening stance of the survivor analyst and how it reflects the inner work of ongoing self-analysis, with regard to the experience of survivorship. The sensitivity and refinement of what Reik (1948) termed the "third ear" may be especially pronounced in post-traumatic survivors. Reik writes:

> One of the peculiarities of this third ear is that it works in two ways. It can catch what other people do not say, but only feel and think; and it can also be turned inward. It can hear voices from within the self that are otherwise not audible because they are drowned out by the noise of our conscious thought processes. The student of psychoanalysis is advised to listen to those inner voices with more attention than to what "reason" tells about the unconscious.
>
> (p. 147)

Overestimating capacities and difficulties setting emotional boundaries

Perhaps it is not surprising that many survivor siblings develop reputations for being clinicians that can handle cases referred to as "difficult," meaning the cases that involve a greater degree of emotional involvement and distress or, in what has come to colloquially take on more pejorative terms, Axis II diagnoses. In my experience, what may initially begin as an unreflective masochistic compliance toward the indiscriminate provision of care can evolve into a mature, individually motivated caretaking, if the right conditions for self-examination continually get met. But the bridge to this seasoned capacity often enough first involves encountering via enactment the omnipotent fantasy of trying to cure others with continuous, impeccable attunement. Thinking relationally, I prefer to focus on the self-state rather than the unconscious wish held within it. This phase of clinical work involves primarily inhabiting an idealized, wise child in the treatment of a patient (Ferenczi, 1923). What others have termed rescue fantasies, I prefer to think of as an activation of the self-state that, from an attachment perspective, was given the most reinforcement relationally within a survivor sibling – that of an idealized, well-resourced caretaker (Schaffer, 2006). Given the autobiographical experience of survivorship in childhood, it is quite natural that many survivor siblings will spend a good deal of time in this self-state of being. I am not challenging the defensive model which locates omnipotence at its heart here, but rather suggesting a less shameful approach toward understanding the functionality of masochism in providing a reflective platform for building bridges toward other states of awareness.

The secondary shame that goes along with feeling that one is wrong for wanting to cure, or believing that they can cure others, does not facilitate integration or the development of less masochistic modes of relatedness. As a rule, interrogation rarely facilitates integration. By focusing on the historical origins of this state, we give survivors a chance to reflect on the experience rather than protect themselves from humiliation. We offer an opportunity to dissolve dissociative barriers rather than unwittingly reinforcing them. We know that shame shuts awareness down and invites further dissociation. So let's listen in as these survivor siblings describe how they made use of inhabiting their "wise child" selves in the service of the work.

Clinical perspectives on boundaries

Marisa, a well-seasoned female analyst with a busy practice, tells me about how she "*stuck it out with a verbally abusive psychotic patient for 18 years,*" acknowledging now that it was "*far longer than might have been good*" for either her or the patient. I notice that 18 years is coincidently also the length of time a parent is legally responsible for the care of a dependent child, and she gives me what I interpret to be a knowing smile in response. In talking about this case, **Marisa** identifies how her inner beleaguered and defective selves were instantly activated by the patient's hostile projections and how these parts of herself tend to "*forget about other kinds of non-harming relations,*" not even knowing there can be an exit. She tells me it's easy for her to forget and to stay in modes of relating that reinforce her sense of defectiveness rather than transmute it. This tendency came to light as she imagined very clearly that another analyst would have called the patient's attention to their cruelty at the time it was happening or possibly ended the treatment far sooner than she had been able to do. In fact, she tells me, it was the patient that ultimately left, as **Marisa** could not allow herself to give up on the treatment. In her own words,

I think I have an abundance of empathy for anyone who feels inadequate because I have been really plagued by insecurity and low self esteem. The problem with this much empathy is that the over-identification can

lead to difficulties in setting limits and boundaries, and left me need-
ing to feel like I was the good one. The worst legacy of all this is how
it robs me of a chance to be in touch with my aggression, and making
use of my bad therapist feelings.

In this illustration, inter-systemic dialogue was not accessible and without access to more parts of her self-experience, **Marisa** was left enacting
rather than transforming her experience of being the exploited wise-child
with no way out. At the time, there was no meditative inner space for her to
reflect on what was being re-enacted, but her discussion of this case past-
tense reveals how she made use of the experience later on.

   Carolyn adopts a pragmatic approach to the work and relays,

Being a survivor sibling is what trained me to be a therapist. I find my
energy has a calming effect on people in the face of strong anxiety
because others pickup that I am not afraid of that in the room. On the
other hand, if strong feelings of helplessness – not worry, but helpless-
ness – get triggered in me, as in I don't know if I can help them or if
they can be helped, I am not ok.

She tells me that this shuts down a meditative space inside as she feels herself getting reactive. Things fall apart at this moment when it is not clear
how permanent a state of mind this sense of unending hopelessness really
is. She tells me she relies on "*deepening*" her engagement here because
she knows if she is being "*deeply impacted,*" it is related to encountering
her own wish for hope that she may "*make a difference*"; "*I can never
escape the hope for growth*" and "*I grow depressed if it's not there.*" For
example, she tells me of a 13-year-long treatment with a male patient:

There are parts of him that remain stuck and unchanged. . . . I can get so
angry and wonder, "Why does he stay there?" I have to deepen my
engagement here, and realize he may have changed as far as he needs
to for him, even though I wish it could be more – but that's about me.

She goes on to tell me, "*so long as my caretaking impulse is reflective
and not reactive, I can do this work and derive a lot of pleasure.*" But
to achieve this equilibrium requires regular self-monitoring. I think this
is where supervision and colleague consultation can be truly instrumental. Talking with a colleague who remains outside the dyadic field can

alleviate the affective press within a reenactment, restoring a broader sense of perspective on what is transpiring. This helps a survivor sibling analyst regain access to other parts of self.

Darlene, an intuitive, confident clinician reflects,

Anytime I have a patient who also has an impaired sibling, it's a moment of identification and many times, they pick up on some way that I am identifying with them and how I can hone in on their being "the normal one." But one time when a patient's story was eerily similar to mine, I was so moved by having a me-too experience that it got in the way of doing the work.

The echoes of her own inner experience being articulated aloud blurred the distinction between self and other and opened up the wound of sibling-longing for her. The boundaries were blurred, leaving her hungering for resonance, and at the time she did not trust that she could (re) establish an internal meta-dialogue. Absent this, the overidentification feels dangerous and like a relationship without boundaries. In this case, she was unable to make use of the blurredness between them and unable to trust it would lead them to someplace they needed to go. Without other self-states present, she could not transmute the longing for resonance into clinical action.

Claire, a practical and attentive clinician tells me,

I've taken to calling Monday's "masochist day" at work. I really identify with my masochistic patients who work so hard to make it easy for those around them. I am a funny mix of very assertive, but assertively masochistic – "who needs what?" I guess it offsets the guilt, some tradeoff as in, "I'll be in charge of your needs and my needs, I'll overfunction for us both."

She elaborates, "*I find it so much harder to sit with no growth. I have feelings of real inadequacy which I can talk myself out of intellectually but that's not my emotional experience of it.*" She quotes Bass (2001) here, saying how treatment can "*endow the event with a feeling of real experience*" (p. 688) but that this is blocked if she's pulled into disidentifying with her own emotional state. Holding badness is a dilemma here too, if it's not in the context of a wider inner dialogue, and becomes all too real as evidence of one's own lack.

With **Kira**, again we see how the wise-child self-state dominates the experience of doing clinical work:

My countertransference experience is often one of too much-ness. There is so much there. In particular, when I was working with a young man who witnessed his sister have a seizure and he was paralyzed and couldn't visit his sister in the hospital, I felt he was very selfish for not going. I am so driven by the omnipotent fantasy of rescue; it's with me always. This goes way back. As a kid I remember thinking, "how would I get all of us out of here if this house were burning?" And for my sister's Confirmation, I was pouring with sweat praying she wouldn't have a seizure there. I have frustration when patients don't live the life I imagine for them, when they don't have any hope. I can be very present emotionally with them. But if they try to sell me on magical thinking, I get very negative about it. Also I notice a lot around my work and my work ethic, an inner voice chides me, "Well my sister couldn't work, so you must get on with it." As kids, none of us, me or my other siblings, addressed what was going on with us internally so it shows up now in my intense countertransference and my rescue fantasies.

The difficulty with boundaries is best understood by a mix-up of internal boundaries within the self-system of the survivor analyst that affects the field between self and patient. If you don't have all your players on the field, so to speak, the game can be interrupted. Without access to one's inner team, the analyst can easily be left feeling that they cannot impact or alter the relatedness between themself and the patient and they must survive it, just like in childhood. It can feel disabling, as there can be a volleying back and forth of who is responsible for this failure. But upon close listening, this condition is at least partially generated by the inner dissociative experience. In each of these instances, we can hear how the survivor sibling analyst is working to bridge in other states of awareness alongside the compulsory caretaker/wise child state. When a meta-dialogue or larger quorum is met, the work continues. But when the compulsive caretaker is left alone in providing the treatment, it more often than not stymies the work. A question emerges of how to use wounded self-states or states of wounding as tools in the treatment itself.

To make this leap, one has to encounter the unexperienced-experience of loss more fully and with more parts of oneself present, or else traumatic reenactment becomes the outcome. The most useful sentence I ever found for creating space internally when it feels for sure lost is written by Micheal Singer (2007) in his book called *The Untethered Soul*. A book centered in spiritual development and consciousness, he says, "What you can do is notice that you noticed" (p. 81). Whatever the disturbance is, the simple act of occupying a position of inner witness already creates a seat apart from the-one-who-is-disturbed or in this case, desperate to 'help.' He goes further to say that "real transformation begins when you embrace your problems as agents for growth" (p. 81). Harris (2009) reminds all analysts that, "clinical momentum is possible when space/time matrix opens in the analyst and when the tumble into the abyss is genuinely possible" (p. 19). Rather than avoid the enactment of singularly powerful self-states with ties to the inner object world, we might as well make use of these moments.

Heightened attunement to loss

Freud's (1917) seminal paper on mourning centered the capacity to consciously move through loss of an object at the heart of psychic health. Survivor siblings are enrolled in a lifelong course in loss. I think psychoanalysis could benefit more from sitting with recognition of loss and its generative and limiting properties. When loss is not inhabited, mourning cannot ensue which severely limits the capacity among the bereft for presence and emotional vitality. The cost to human subjectivity can be great. Loss may be conceptualized as an ongoing internal experience that goes beyond any single event, person, or points in time that can adversely impact development, symbolization, resiliency, and health. You could review a transcript of any psychotherapy session and realize just how much loss is the focus of our inner psychic dialogues – whether it's made implicit or explicit, whether it's in relation to a part of self, another person, an inner object, a place, an experience, or time itself. The loss of time, loss of ability to connect with one-selves or across self-states, loss of imagination, loss of capacity to be with others in a mutual way, loss of the experience of encountering loss, loss of actual loved ones, and the loss inherent in separation, are all parts of the human experience at one time or another. I find myself really puzzled at clinical presentations when someone says something like, "this was their first loss" or "they don't have any experience with loss." It's simply not possible to get through life without an experience of loss. I think what differentiates survivor siblings in this regard is the readiness to attune to loss as it manifests in conscious and unconscious experience. The prime is pumped.

Inhabiting loss actually breeds contact and presence, but it can be so frightening and destabilizing to go into it that most of us do not realize that presence and connectivity await us on the other side of mourning. Doing clinical work invites the experience of loss directly into one's life. We hear about our patients' losses as our own losses are activated, and we facilitate a process of change, which inherently is accompanied by loss, even when it is toward health that the patient moves. Have you ever noticed the dreams patients bring in as their own internal worlds get transformed? While there is often exhilaration and joy, there can be real mourning, in letting go of specific defensive maneuvers or with the modification of internal objects, so that even when these changes are desired, a loss accompanies it. It's not uncommon to hear patients describe different landscapes, construction sites, and metaphors depicting the internal change. It's less common for analysts to make room for patients to mourn the dissociative and defensive structures as they undergo modification through treatment.

As a personal example, nothing brought the centrality of loss home to me further than giving birth to my son. Fortunately, my labor was non-traumatic and I gave birth to a healthy child. At a time when I imagined I would feel nothing but joy, there was also loss. There was a sense within my younger selves of surprise because they did not anticipate that parenting would be one long, lifetime exercise in letting-go, separating, and losing the constancy of at-oneness that pregnancy ensured in a bodily way. Of course, sustaining at oneness is not only undesirable but also impossible since the bliss of togetherness can only occur by our very separation. But from my inner child's point of view, it was quite a shock to feel that becoming a parent also meant mastering and accepting saying goodbye as well as hello. I am not alone in this. Many survivor siblings seem to attend to the nuanced ways in which loss shapes human experience in their patient's lives and within the treatment over time.

Clinical perspectives on loss

Harold, a clinician deeply in touch with the loss of his brother, uses his awareness of body communications and considers deeply the sibling experience of all his patients, whether they are explicitly discussing it or not. He tells me,

I have a very dissociated patient who is the oldest of 7 siblings, whom he took care of growing up. He doesn't notice, but I hear how he draws on child-rearing metaphors very often to describe seemingly unrelated experiences. The caretaker part of him is constantly mourning even if he doesn't notice it.

Harold realizes that his patient is communicating through this metaphor a disavowed loss of his own childhood, as the eldest caretaker to a house full of younger kids. **Harold**'s sensitivity to loss conditions him to hone in on the recurrence of this theme in his patient's speech. As awareness of premature loss and separation occupy his countertransference experience, this degree of sensitivity can be a real gift to patients who may be apt to minimize or not notice the ways they feel, or have lost out on certain relationships and experiences.

 Rachel, an unobtrusive female therapist with a maternal presence tells me,

It's hard for me to conceptualize how this experience impacts my clinical work because it's not conscious. Often times there will be a mentally ill sibling in the life of my patient and I remember, in the beginning of my practice, I did not initially get the difference because I naively assumed the picture of a sibling with a mental illness would be like my sister, in it's unpredictability, out of control behavior, loss, etc. This blotted out the ways in which it was different because I too readily identified with how the well-off sibling felt. For example, I readily understood how my patients identified with the stories of their parents, how closely they attended to the parents' inner experiences, and with the responsibility to be the healthy sibling, what it's like to be leaned on for support by one's own parents. This setup some transference/countertransference paradigms, where the patient represented younger me, and I slipped in and out of a parental transference, where I could more easily identify with what the parents felt and vacate the spot of healthy sibling, which for them/me obviously just recreates the experience of being overlooked. One female patient [I treated] whose twin was very low functioning and chronically disabled, . . . [kept describing to me].her mother's investment in the twin's care and advocacy – I could notice the ways she was not attending to her mom's absence. But I'm not sure I considered how that would replay between us in the transference/ countertransference until we were knee deep in it.

Sometimes what exists outside of consciousness can only be discovered when it gets re-enacted and reactivated between the patient and the therapist. Rachel's overidentification with the patient set the patient up to feel a maternal absence. Because even though they have had similar experiences, it was not the same experience.

Hannah, an intuitive and relatable therapist, tells me that she is able to "*work with patients at the basic fault, the place where they first felt too small to handle that which the world was giving them.*" She relays,

In my own inner work, in a state of deep concentration and reverie, I enter into a body experience of being in the NICU incubator separated from my disabled twin for the first time and recall this effort to make the next breath happen, along with the feeling "where is he?" In my clinical work, this reverie is there and let's me understand abandonment issues, dissociation, all those things, in an experience near way. . . . My survivorship informs me in ways I don't even know. I have a patient whose child has a seizure disorder and I'm able to be compassionate with her, and gently notice the ways she's accommodated it, and I don't think I could have done so without my experience of my brother.

In particular, she tells me that she appreciates how dissociation allows the mom to go on functioning, but that in the treatment, **Hannah** holds the door open for curiosity about the impact such selective attention has on her patient's sense of self.

Debra, a thoughtful and bright analyst, shares that survivorship shows up in her affective experience.

It's not that uncommon for me to find myself really anxious with a patient or after being with one. One way or another, the theme of being "sent away" gets activated in the clinical encounter. Sometimes it's literally in a story a patient is telling me, but sometimes I'm aware of my wish to get rid of someone and the masochistic reaction formation to evade the experience of being the privileged sibling that accompanies it. I have trouble then setting limits – it would be truly crippling to do this work if I hadn't been heard by my analyst. I am more attuned to the sibling dimension. My institute is a bit classical, so I was trained to hear competition and to think Oedipally. But I very often hear the sibling competition – who is going to get what resources as opposed to who is winning. I think I am able to hear it differently, this lateral dimension. I also think that the guilt of mourning someone who was lost but alive, makes survivor siblings good at handling death, even in cases of so called more straight forward mourning.

Debra goes on to tell me,

For me, patient growth is relatively uncomplicated and pleasurable, [there's] a real gratification in it for me. [I remember] a case from a long time ago – a woman who was very depressed, the oldest and responsible sibling, with early mother loss, she needed to do more mourning on this loss, which she knew about and I watched her experience me as maternal and work her way through these feelings and memories. I don't think I did much but she came out the other end solid. I think I feel relieved when people feel better, otherwise I'm left with "I'm a Charlatan who takes peoples money but I don't help."

Debra relies on supervision for those cases that put her in contact with fear – fear of not helping and fear of being complicit in receiving compensation from patients who show no evidence of benefitting from the analytic relationship she offers. Supervision gives her the space to analyze her fear instead of react to it.

Evolving experiences with growth

One thematic area ripe for demonstrating how the inner experience of a survivor sibling may contribute to the listening stance involves growth. Growth is a particularly charged area since it draws into focus the experience of loss held within the lateral dimension. Survivor siblings grow in size, physicality, mind, and spirit, while their disabled sibling's growth is constricted by medical necessity. On the surface, it would seem survivor siblings might then celebrate change and development in their clinical work, but underneath change brings a season of loss and separation. Sitting with patients can unwittingly place one in contact with the actual spatial gap between oneself and one's disabled sibling, ushering in the solitary environment that so often characterizes this kind of survivorship.

The responses to solitariness and loss are varied, but often enough one is initially polarized into overinvestment or underinvestment in a patient's growth as a way of protecting oneself. Of course, contemporary perspectives include the patient's contribution in co-determining which state of mind the analyst resonates with and when. But for the purpose of this chapter, I am attempting to highlight how the very phenomena one is trying to help a patient work out (e.g., their unconscious response and reactions to loss) must first be gone through, each time anew, by the analyst vis-á-vis their patient through the transference/countertransference medium. Both parties must attend to their ambivalent feelings toward growth as it happens.

Even still, a generative enactment is not inherently promised to any of us. Psychic growth and its absence in our patients and us can easily reopen the wound of difference between survivor siblings and their disabled siblings, disabling the analyst to make use of the experience in the present. In some ways, no position is ever comfortable. Whether you experience yourself as equipped to handle things your patient cannot yet manage or struggle to do so, the loneliness encountered in being apart from the other person, and the sense of responsibility that goes along with creating a treatment context meant to facilitate growth, can awaken an awareness of one's own wounds in less than obvious ways. The joy at "being found" is ever elusive.

It's the premise of this book that the more we are able to tolerate inhabiting unexperienced-experience with more of ourselves present, the more we ultimately evolve. The lessons held in the vacated experience can be absorbed, enriching and modifying our inner landscape, which necessarily changes our relationship to both loss and growth. Let's now turn to some examples that illustrate these transformational moments.

Clinical perspectives on growth

Susan, a dedicated therapist, shared with me an unpublished paper she had written about her experience treating a patient who passed away in her young adult years from a terminal illness. **Susan** maintained the treatment with this patient, up to the very end, and shared how when speech was no longer possible, she slipped back into a way of communicating she had used with her own sibling, who is also now deceased. Her patient's ultimate passing and the memories it elicited for **Susan** regarding her own disabled siblings untimely death, posed an opportunity for her to revisit and revise some of her dissociative strategies for managing this past pain, as it became present again through her intense clinical encounter. While she did not share her own biographical experience directly with this patient, or with others that came to mind when I asked her about her experience of working as an analyst, we can assume that in a relational sense, she absolutely shared this early experience of her own survivorship in the ways she attended to the varying levels of communication around life and death matters – how she maintained her role of participant witness and how early life uniquely prepared her to be someone who could do this for a patient who was dying. In her own words, she tells me,

In my early years, I was so blindly interested in patient growth. I think over time I have disinvested myself of this outcome and appreciate when patient's grow, but can reflect on when they don't.

She attributes this to having the help of a strong supervisor who relieved her of the impulse to cure and helped clarify what she is and is not responsible for in the treatment.

Olina, a generous and soft-spoken therapist, shares her own process:

A big one for me is fear of abandonment, I felt emotionally abandoned by my parents and carried this core belief that "if I don't give people what they want or need, they will leave me" right into the work. It's very hard for me to catch it happening in real time, but I know it shows up. For example, I find I may block opportunities for patients to be angry at me. . . . I avoid risking that they might leave me and try to allow for that space to be there. . . . When patients do grow it feels really satisfying, this feeling that I helped with that. But actually it can also bring up abandonment, "will this person still chose me if they get better? What is my value and worth? What does it mean for me to ask that challenging question or to sit in the silence a little longer?" When growth is absent I think, "why isn't change happening here. Am I not really understanding them?". . .[For example, I had a male patient who was] so depressed for so long. I liked him, but [he was] not easy to be with – very cynical and had to be disparaging of the therapy. . . . My inner process sounded like, "Wow what can I do? I can't help this person get out of the hole." I was trapped so much through childhood and adolescence – I struggle with it, in the ways I still keep myself trapped. Am I allowed to be good? To succeed at something by walking away?

Selena, a kind and wise therapist, shares,

The biggest issue for me is this chronic low self-esteem. Whenever my patients need to be close to me, the first thing that happens in my head, "am I valuable, am I going to be enough to help them?" I don't have problems being very close to people in the moment of their suffering. I can be close when they are in pain, but if they are happy or defensive or both, my insecurity appears. . . . I try to ground myself, in the necessity of talking and showing people the kinds of messages they are unconsciously signaling to others in their lives, but it's hard.

She shares that when patients are *"not growing, I feel a lot of guilt. I can celebrate growth in a self-conscious way, but its absence is haunting."* The loss of self-esteem and self-worth can help and hurt her in her experience of being a therapist.

Rose, with a quiet yet strong presence, tells me,

If I have a patient who feels out of control emotionally in the room, like uninhibited, it freaks me out. I am especially allergic to patients who are in crisis, who need me more. I am sure I discourage it because I resent their needing me.

But upon reflection, we realized this had more to do with the caretaking of her mom than her sibling. Because ultimately,

Growth is exciting, it makes me feel good. This work is so painstaking and long and it can be hard for long periods of time to know that what I am doing is actually making a difference . . . I think about all the ways in which I relate to myself and other people and how much has changed.

It really is a remarkable thing that human relationships have the capacity to transform lives. **Rose** reflects, *"Sometimes I grow envious of my chiropractor, who can have this immediate effect and make me feel better."* On the other hand, she says, *"I can handle non-growth, I'm a little dissociated from it, but I remind myself, this is the nature of the work and I don't tend to feel overly responsible for it."*

However, much we may wish to not feel responsible for our patient's growth, a survivor sibling's self-states may have different and contradictory ideas about taking or forfeiting such responsibility. **Darlene** shares,

I have a low tolerance for dependency issues, when [female] patients put up with men who feel like a drag and can't get themselves together. [I think there is] fear of dependency happening here, and what it means to take care of the "sick one," I don't think there's anyone who doesn't deserve to be spoken to as a human being. I look at the non-verbal communication to work out of this space. It's not a linear thing, it happens in such nuanced ways. I'm thinking of my work with this very schizoid patient, who one day said to me, "It feels cold in here, can you turn the heat up?" One can speak and it won't damage the relationship. I feel really proud when patients discover this in my care. When they aren't growing, my frustration mounts . . . you can do better than this.

Darlene switches from an awareness of her frustration with female patients who attach themselves to chronically dependent partners, into a self-state which identifies with that very same position.

Regarding hopelessness, **Rachel** described her work with a fragile patient living a high-risk life within a borderline mental state:

The hopelessness in me, it's really profound. She can't be helped – there's just a block, experiencing her as so limited and so inaccessible. . . [is] very painful for me. At one point, I felt hopeful that I had cracked it. I felt I had made a connection with her – but her distress, similar to my sister's cognitive impairment, meant I could never really tell or trust how far our connection would take her because you are always uncertain, not knowing where you are with someone who can't tell you directly about the ways in which they have internalized this mutuality. It started to feel very similar. I was left with questioning, "how far can this relationship go? How much should I hope she can take me in?

The questions of capacity are daunting and painful. On growth, she relates,

I initially feel positive and proud, but always in the back of my mind, I'm skeptical – like waiting for the other shoe to drop. This is a wonderful moment, but horror is coming! Makes it hard to relish it, but it also

protects me as I walk through my practice more tolerant of failures and disappointments. I guess there is just this unreality to change and growth. People are complex. Chaos and destruction come to feel more real. Things fall apart, these are all ways of coping for me.

Conclusion

Ongoing self-analysis and remaining receptive to inhabiting the unexperienced-experience within survivorship can transmute what would otherwise be an analyst's blind spot(s) (or a singular wounded self-state experience) into a mediated space of meta-dialogue, a source of therapeutic action. A pan-psychic outlook "locate(s) recognition as a process in which transitional space is realized precisely as a consequence of the experienced distinction between internal and external worlds having in some measure been transcended" (Brown, 2020, p. 88). Nothing is inherent though, it requires a disciplined practice of paying attention. And though the practice itself has no end point, that doesn't mean it's not constantly evolving into a greater capacity to be present when there is effort. There is an art and surrender involved in paying attention and listening inside and outside simultaneously. In knowing where to go or what to do to re-establish the inner meta-dialogue when it's lost. Benatar (2004) writes:

> Re-enactments in the context of trauma transferences engage the therapist in very specific, usually intense ways. It is my argument that these kinds of engagements with patients that activate their primitive early childhood attachment needs, will or can evoke the attachment system of the therapist, and can bring about positive change in the therapist's self-system.
>
> (p. 13)

Not only do survivor siblings offer up the capacity to both heal and wound their patients in the ways they were both healed and wounded, their efforts on this front also affect the generations to come. In the next chapter, we will consider some of the intergenerational inheritances of survivorship.

References

Apprey, M. (2014). Containing the uncontainable: The return of the phantom and its reconfiguration in ethnonational conflict resolution. *The American Journal of Psychoanalysis, 74*(2), 162–175.

Aron, L. (1996). *A meeting of minds: Mutuality in psychoanalysis*. Routledge.

Bass, A. (2001). It takes one to know one; Or, whose unconscious is it anyway? *Psychoanalytic Dialogues, 11*(5), 683–702.

Benatar, M. (2004). Purification and the self-system of the therapist. *Trauma & Dissociation, 5*(4), 1–15.

Bollas, C. (1979). The transformational object. *International Journal of Psycho-Analysis, 60*, 97–107.

Brown, R. (2020). *Groundwork for a transpersonal psychoanalysis: Spirituality, relationship and participation*. Routledge.

Dobrich, J. (2020). An elegy for motherless daughters: Multiplicity, mourning & dissociation. *Psychoanalytic Perspectives, 7*(3). 366–384.

Faimberg, H. (2005). *The telescoping of generations: Listening to the narcissistic links between generations*. Routledge.

Farber, S. K. (Ed.). (2017). *Celebrating the wounded healer psychotherapist: Pain, post-traumatic growth and self-disclosure*. Routledge.

Ferenczi, S. (1923). The dream of the "learned infant." *International Journal of Medical Psychoanalysis, IX*, 70.

Flax, M. (2011). A crisis in the analyst's life: Self-containment, symbolization, and the holding space. *Psychoanalysis Quarterly, 80*(2), 305–336.

Freud, S. (1917). Mourning and melancholia. In *The standard edition of the complete psychological works of Sigmund Freud, volume XIV (1914–1916): On the history of the psycho-analytic movement: Papers on metapsychology and other works* (pp. 237–258). London and Hogarth Press.

Gabbard, G. O. (1989). On 'doing nothing' in the psychoanalytic treatment of the refractory borderline patient. *International Journal of Psycho-Analysis, 70*, 527–534.

Harris, A. (2009). You must remember this. *Psychoanalytic Dialogues, 19*(1), 2–21.

Harris, A., Kalb, M., & Klebanoff, S. (2016). *Ghosts in the consulting room: Echoes of trauma in psychoanalysis*. Routledge.

Hopenwasser, K. (2008). Being in rhythm: Dissociative attunement in the therapeutic process. *Journal of Trauma and Dissociation, 9*(3), 349–367.

Khan, M. R. (1963). Silence as communication. *Bulletin of the Menninger Clinic, 27*, 300–313.

Kuchuck, S. (2014). *Clinical implications of the psychoanalyst's life experience: When the personal becomes professional*. Routledge.

Ogden, T. (1994). The concept of interpretive action. *The Psychoanalytic Quarterly, 63*(2), 219–245.

Reik, T. (1948). *Listening with the third ear*. Farrar, Straus and Giroux.

Ruderman, E. J. (2002). As time goes by: Life experiences and their effects on analytic technique. *Psychoanalytic Inquiry, 22*, 495–509.

Schaffer, A. (2006). The analyst's curative fantasies. *Contemporary Psychoanalysis, 42*(3), 349–366.

Schore, A. N. (1994). *Affect regulation and the origin of the self*. Routledge.

Searles, H. F. (1975). The patient as therapist to his analyst. In P. Giovacchini (Ed.), *Tactics and techniques in psychoanalytic Theory*. Jason Aronson.

Singer, M. (2007). *The untethered soul: The journey beyond yourself*. New Harbinger Publications.

Sloane, J. A. (2017). Wounded healer, healing wounder: A personal story. In S. Farber (Ed.), *Celebrating the wounded healer psychotherapist: Pain, post-traumatic growth and self-disclosure* (pp. 201–207). Routledge.

Slochower, J. (1996). *Holding and psychoanalysis: A relational Perspective*. The Analytic Press.

Slochower, J. (2013). Psychoanalytic mommies & psychoanalytic babies. *Contemporary Psychoanalysis*, *49*(4), 606–628.

Stern, D. B. (2019). *The infinity of the unsaid: Unformulated experience, language and the non-verbal*. Routledge.

Stevens, A. (1994). *Jung: A very short introduction*. Oxford University Press.

Winnicott, D. W. (1958). The capacity to be alone. *International Journal of Psycho-Analysis*, *39*, 416–420.

Chapter 8

Transgenerational impacts

We know arrested grief gets relived generationally, so we have to put words to things that perhaps our parents have not.

– Debra

We've got it wrong that a story starts with a birth and ends with a death. The story is so much longer than that. A single subject's life is made up of all the experiences that precede and follow them, as they get transmitted both consciously and unconsciously across time through relationships. As individuals, we may only be consciously privy to our own experience and some of the generation before and after us, but unconsciously, what we carry has no limit. One of the most important turns in recent theorizing that cuts across disciplines of psychological study has been the consideration of transgenerational experience on psychic identity, as it gets passed through the micro-medium of family and the macro-medium of culture and "Big History" (Grand & Salberg, 2017b). Pauline Boss's (1999) research on the impact of ambiguous loss across family timelines and the haunting experience encapsulated by Grand and Salberg's (2017a) *Transgenerational Trauma & the Other*, an edited collection looking at the intersection of cultural trauma and individual identity, are both illustrations of this important turn in our collective clinical theorizing. Within this collection, Salberg and Grand focus on the repair of these wounds through witnessing. In another important piece on transgenerational trauma, Gerson (2009) illustrates how trauma is compounded when the place from which to witness is "dead."

An attachment perspective is apt here because attachment is the vehicle in which trauma may be transmitted. The caregiving dyad may be parent to child, analyst to analysand, candidate to supervisor, student to instructor, and so on. It is the gaps and absence, not the presence of mediated conflict and strain, which contaminate the next generation. Siegel shows how incoherence in attachment, characterized by incongruity, fragmentation, and a restricted flow of information is contagious within relationships (p. 313). So in attending to these micro- and macro-inheritances, we want to assess and monitor the attachment system for coherence (both inside the survivor as it represents their self-system and between/within caregiving dyads). The ability to inhabit, think about, reflect on, struggle with, and maintain what I have elsewhere termed a meta-dialogue (Dobrich, 2020), both within the self-system of a survivor and more broadly within our psychoanalytic communities with respect to survivorship and the sibling dimension, delineates the conditions of which the next-generation inherits.

One way of considering a survivor sibling is to think of them as patient zero for this particular haunting. The survivor sibling carries the ghostly presence of the lost healthy sibling/lost healthy sibling relationship/lost healthy sense of self/selves, lost idealized parent/s vis-à-vis this encounter within their psychic identity. All those who interact with them are apt to be touched by their survivorship in one way or another. The question isn't if, but how the impact is felt and transmitted. Boss (1999) writes, "The devastation wrought by unresolved grief is only intensified when no one validates it" (p. 59). But a psychoanalytic perspective recognizes that this validation must be an internal one in addition to a familial and cultural one. Let's consider and formulate some of the imagined and elaborated upon micro- and macro-transgenerational impacts of survivor siblings, within their individual familial lives as well as within the larger professional realm of the psychoanalytic community.

Micro-reflections: survivor siblings as parents

I intentionally left the last question of my interview open-ended to leave room for subjects to identify and elaborate on things I did not think to ask about, with regard to the experience of survivorship. While not all participating subjects are parents, those who are spoke to their experience of parenting. Many shared stories of their inner reveries of their own parenting experience as well as their encounters of watching their children interact as siblings. When a dissociative structure predominates the self-system, survivorship makes itself known through hauntings and gaps, which are often felt by the next generation, who has no way of understanding the origins of such lacunas. In turn, because children are developmentally ego-centric and reliant on their caregivers, they are likely to imagine the "bad stuff" held within these "gaps" has something to do with them personally. Thus, the cycle of perpetuating insecure and disorganized attachments is continued, as these impressionable children absorb their parent's dissociative projections. But when a survivor engages in healing, perhaps "earning" a secure attachment status within their self-system through treatment, the way survivorship impacts the next generation is modified because the internal structure of the survivor has changed. Personally, I am buoyed in the clinical work by knowing that "creating coherence is a lifetime project. Integration is thus a process, not a final accomplishment" (Siegel, 1999, p. 336). It feels true that there is no end point in time to this process, and yet it also feels true that you can feel the difference of being haunted by survivorship and ultimately developing a capacity to bear being with that experience as it was/is.

On feeling haunted as a result of the long-term evasion of unexperienced-experience of survivorship **Harold** tells me:

I remember when I first became a parent myself, I recall everyone getting into the car, including my wife at the time. I was suddenly overcome with a feeling that someone was missing from the car. Was it our German Shepard? But it gradually dawned on me that I was feeling my then deceased brother's presence decades later, it was a ghost-like intrusion at the time.

The dislocation and not fully inhabited-yet-encountered experience continues for him as he reflects back:

I think about my parenting role because of having sons too, and the extent to which they have these brotherly relationships. I'm envious, I feel left out. I always have this sense of missing a person, often at family gatherings at my grandparents. I've always had a kind of creepy feeling there. That being together no matter the occasion is mixed up with being like, a shiva call, and accentuates for me [his] absence.

We can hear how he is working to inhabit the unexperienced-experience of growing up alongside his severely disabled brother and losing him in adolescence to death. It shows up in how he experiences events in the present tense, as though he were back in time, missing out on things he never had, watching his own children interact freely. This was a common reverie held among survivor sibling parents – that of looking in on the next generation, from the perspective of lonely inner child.

Rachel shares with me:

My two girls are pretty close in age, and daily I'm encountered with the potential and actual sibling experience they have with each other that I never had. If I can observe it and see what it feels like, it's like wow, I feel so fortunate. I almost overvalue that they have each other, and I have trouble with the meanness of differentiation, the shunning of the younger one by the older one. I think back to my mom telling us how me and my other non-disabled sibling are going to be best friends," how she needed this for herself. But it didn't come true for us. But my kids have it.

Rachel engages more than one feeling in observing her children interact freely among their equally abled selves, implying the presence of more than just the lonely inner child self-state perspective. But I immediately notice that her inner child has a voice in her reverie and is not silent or split off. That's one way that coherence looks among survivors: Having access to the places in which the loss lives on, alongside more present-based perspectives; holding the past and present together, we might say. We might imagine her children experientially feel her wish for them to have no conflict and closeness as *coming from her and about her*, not who they must be, as she also allows them to be who they are with each other. There is something open about the way in which she can differentiate then-and-there from here-and-now and use the affective longings that her daily encounters with her children stir toward the provision of recognition inside herself rather than projecting it upon them.

As the dissociation around the unexperienced-experience of survivorship gets chipped away at, a capacity to inhabit self-states that occupy more of a depressive position takes shape. **Kira** tells me:

My first son was born with a mild deformity. We found out during my pregnancy that he had this abnormality. And that was the year after my [disabled] sister died. And so, that made my son a different baby – a baby with special needs. But it has made me a different mother, where I don't want to have this lived experience of us not speaking about his difference, I want him to know, "Yes you can do everything, but yes I understand there are days where you wish you had another hand," so it's changed my mothering, being aware of my own experience as a child. Being as non-defensively open to it without treating it as a black and white event. I don't know if I would have held this tension of having and not having together, had I not had the experience with my own sister growing up.

Kira readily makes use of the inhabitation of unexperienced-experience by holding the tension together – this disability is a disability, but it's not *only* a disability – transforming the kind of parent she may be through active engagement of various inner perspectives. She does not try to resolve the contradiction, it's just there. I can relate to this, too. Coherent multiplicity rarely feels like a neat, uniform process. For example, I notice just how much self-talk goes into my parenting process, maybe not more so than typical for a first-time parent, but content wise, it's very much informed by a loss-averse strategy. My wise child protector is always there, operating, believing if I can imagine the danger, I can protect us. I have to really reel it in and not imagine a kind of permanent disability or crisis befalling my own child during points of actual physical injury/illness or transient stress in my life. It seems especially heightened around bodily harm. I have witnessed parent friends let their kids fall and not startle and I've had to untrain myself from a startle response, knowing that in my imagination, the way I avoid prospective injury by worrying is actually causing an injury to my son, crippling his sense of open-ended exploration. I don't want him to inherit my fear. Of course, rationally, I know my son can't just acquire a chronic developmental disorder, but again rationality is rarely something that protects a survivor sibling's unconscious life against threat. It's like some part of me is always dreading or expecting that I'll have to live "that life again," the life experience as a survivor sibling during childhood, while other parts of me are aware of how different things are in the present tense. It's with me too, in considering having more children: What if something happened to the next baby? What if my first-born was catapulted into an experience of survivorship? Here too, it takes effort to not make a decision based on fear.

Susan shares:

I think in terms of my own relational symptoms, I carry extraordinary worry about the survival of my own children. And it's like, oh gosh.

I knew there is a degree of normalcy in that, but I think that in my gut
I have always been way overboard, and even when I can say "oh gosh,
that's just your childhood exposure to living against fighting death for
13 years, and warding off death by never talking about it." It helps
some. But I live in this kind of race with mortality.

The impact of enacted rather than reflective caregiving on survivor sibling's life partners, children, friends, and others is a very real and understandable outcome of living in proximity to death and illness during one's formative years. It is also a consequence of having to raise one's most damaged inner parts by yourself internally. Meta-dialogue and ownership of all of one's parts that played a role in the experience can make fighting and tolerating feelings necessary for reflectivity to be possible, which inherently serves the parenting process. But unmediated, these experiences can wreck inner havoc on the relational worlds we build in the present. I think healing does not mean we transcend enactment, it just means we take responsibility and catch ourselves, after or during, a time when we realize it's happened.

Micro-reflections: survivor siblings as siblings & peers

The difficultly and strained relatedness between nondisabled siblings within families was an area that came up in many of the interviews. I did not explicitly ask about this either, the omission itself probably telling. More than a few respondents spoke with a sense of shame and sadness about the strained relationship they had to their other non-disabled siblings. The regret and loss of these other prospective ties only compounded the grief of other losses. In some ways, the shame was heaviest here because with the parents and the disabled sibling, there were concrete observable reasons to explain why connecting fully was "hard." But among siblings of equal capacities, how were they to understand the dislocation and disconnection? At first glance, it may not seem clear why impairment in connection among similarly abled siblings occurs within these families. Growing up around unexperienced-experience with others is an intensely strange and affecting occurrence that has an ahistorical kind of quality to it. There is a sense of there being too much content, too many events that saturate, with too few subjects present to bear witness to the experience, as it unfolds. Or an inner sense of subjectivity that cannot be shared with others. In thinking about this, I called on Sue Grand's (2000) knowledge of what she calls, the "bestiality of survival" (p. 93). She writes:

> The bestial gesture may entail a real act of betrayal, exploitation, violence . . . or may entail a relatively benign feeling, thought or bodily function that the victim experiences as a moral transgression against the self or others.
>
> (p. 93)

The dissociative strategies inherent in being a survivor sibling often entail splitting of the self and relating in depersonalized or depersonalizing ways as children to one another. Even the people-pleasing self is not felt to be the whole truth internally and shame always accompanies a split in self. Large periods of life may be spent surviving, in which operations may typically be run from a more paranoid-schizoid emotional plane, and later on, these ways of being can come to feel like a bestial gesture to the survivor who utilize/d/s them.

A consequence of survivorship is that the very thing you need to do to survive may cause damage to the kinds of other relationships one might have had, had they had greater access to the full range of themselves at the time. The unconscious allegiance to not disrupting the familial equilibrium, or even to those siblings who become the "bad one" within their family system, results in varying degrees of dissociation as this quality of unrealness comes to permeate the whole familial experience. In this context of survival, siblings may have acted and behaved in ways they later come to feel ashamed by. These bestial gestures, both real and imagined, whether explicitly encoded behaviorally or internally experienced through felt-tendencies or subjective absence, make it very difficult to have and sustain closeness to others on the scene at the time, because being close means inhabiting an experience full of shame, fear, and loss head-on. Sibling relations are not excluded from this. As one interviewee put it, "*I regret that I never had a good relationship with my surviving sister. It's been very embattled, we maintain our peace by avoiding each other.*"

While I do not have an embattled relationship with my younger brother, I would not say that we were able to bond or be close around this part of our experience of family life. As I was writing the book, and nearly twenty years after leaving my childhood home, my younger brother and I had the following conversation:

Brother: I went to see our (disabled) brother yesterday at the institution. He seemed really alert, like he really knew who I was. Do you think he knows who we are? Like how does he recognize us, as we get older and look different?

Me: I think he does. I mean, it's the dilemma always, how do we know what we know about what he knows . . . without language? But I like to think attachment is a powerful organizer of his experience, and he uses senses, like the way a small child might not understand the words, but hears the music of our tone and can place who we are/how we feel, and that he may use his other senses, such as sight, smell, and feeling in recognizing us. But I don't really know.

Brother: Yeah, we don't really know. I just don't visit that often. And I wonder if I look different, if he knows me? But he definitely seemed to this time. It was cool; I hadn't seen him that alert in a long time.

We are in our thirties and forties, and this is the first candid conversation I can recall him and I having about the realities of our brother's condition, particularly regarding the sorts of questions it leaves us with regarding recognition and mutuality. It's not that we never spoke of our brother's condition itself before, or even our imagined observations of our parent's experience of it. But I do not have a memory of us talking together in this more *enlivened* way, where we openly acknowledge the limits of our understanding about what our disabled brother's experience is like, and even more so, what it leaves us feeling in response. To talk like this is to transgress my mother's effort at pretending to know exactly what our disabled brother's experience is without question. Wandering in a space of openly not knowing together felt like breaking new ground – ground that could not be broken when we were kids as we submitted to my mom's rendering of our brother. Being so candid together now seems related to his knowledge of my writing the book. It's opened up a space for us to talk about something that has always existed nonverbally between us and within us. The silence that surrounds so much of survivorship begins to crumble as words fall from our mouths onto this page.

Recently at a dinner table of friend's from childhood, I listened to how each person catalogued aspects of their adult lives, including current siblingship stories. Absent an experience of survivorship, I have noticed with longing the ways in which sibling talk appears to be more competitive and compassion-driven. Seemingly siblings talk to each other, about each other, and to other people about one another. It is not unusual for survivor siblings to not reference their sibling experience at all, let alone to regularly talk with one another. Survivor siblings, for all the reasons mentioned so far, lack the ease and freedom to do so. Carrying an inner sense of duplicity in being (mis)perceived the "lucky one" alongside the inner not-so lucky feelings, compromises relatedness within individuals and across family relations. Most interviewees indicated that their relationship with other nondisabled siblings only gradually landed them in a verbal terrain, where they were actively discussing their experiences vis-à-vis their disabled sibling, and it was exclusively in adulthood. This was not a finding I initially expected to encounter, thanks to shame; naturally, I was feeling that I was alone in this.

Macro-reflections: finding a place for siblings in psychoanalysis

A search for "siblings" in PepWeb returns 55 hits compared to the 277 hits when searching for "parents." This unevenness in attentiveness, the implicit avoidance of peer and lateral relations as a serious point of study or concern in the discipline of psychoanalysis itself, does not seem incidental. We might go so far as to say it occupies a dissociative gap in our collective psyche. Harris et al. (2016) write: "What is wounding about experience, what may corrupt our reason and hurt us past what seems bearable, is that which imagination cannot modify and transfigure" (p. 137). We cannot transform that which remains unseen and unimagined. As psychoanalysts, we know that silence and avoidance can signify an enactment of the paranoid/schizoid dissociative defense that blocks meaning-making and inhibits a depressive position (Ogden, 1989). Often enough it means something is too threatening to take form or be considered in thought. It begs the question, what's so threatening about considering this dimension of human experience as clinicians and thinkers? The silence around siblings may represent, in part, a fear that empowering lateral relations displaces the primacy of the older generation. Fears of mortality and the wish to remain instrumental may be shown in an unthought-known commitment to epistemological orientations that privilege power relations between parents and children on the collective level. As argued earlier, perhaps the stance was initially adopted out of loyalty to (the father) Freud and not (the brother/mother) Ferenczi (Berman, 2004). Safer's (2002) book on siblings begins with the acknowledgment that: "'Siblings' does not appear in the 404-page index to the twenty-three-volume *Standard Edition of Freud*" (p. 29). Or maybe this contemporary failure to imagine siblingship is rooted in other unformulated experiences, not yet inhabitable?

The first step to formulation is noticing the lacuna. More recently this gap in knowledge has come into focus. Within the Relational world, the experience of peer relatedness is getting conceptualized in unique academic ways. I think of Aron's (2018) chapter on inhabiting a reflexive skepticism through ambivalence as an apt metaphor for peer-to-peer relations among varying psychoanalytic schools of orientation, as one model for showing the generative impact between siblings. Similarly, Grand's (2018) focus on resiliency and looking beyond the primary caregiving dyad into other relational spaces, including peer relatedness, is another. Juliet Mitchell (2000, 2003), who theorizes a place for siblings in our unconscious life through her work, has not to my knowledge been incorporated in psychoanalytic curriculums to the extent that we might expect. In a Relational consideration of intimacies, Cornell (2013) and Clough (2013) both center lateral experience at the heart of growing self-awareness and explain how typical registration of power between parents and children can preclude and foreclose the development of sibling intimacies.

Historically speaking, emphasis is often placed on passing the torch from one generation of clinical thinkers to the next, as opposed to what gets born between peers and siblings. What may be discovered and encountered from *within* cohorts is starting to take shape in our clinical papers and presentations. With so much emphasis placed on generational inheritances, we may be apt to miss the ways in which side-by-side encounters effect the self and the field more generally. But again, this is changing. A concurrent growth in knowledge regarding the impact of trauma on subjectivity along with an emphasis on lateral spaces is an exciting frontier for psychoanalysis to dive into.

Adoption of a trauma-informed developmental approach that inspires psychoanalysts to experience both enactments and impasses as opportunities to transform unexperienced-experience, especially as it pertains to lateral life, might be more readily included within our psychoanalytic curriculums and clinical journals. In discussing gradations of experience, Stein (2019) identifies "the experience itself, the meaning event, and the effect on consciousness" (p. 12). With trauma, the experience itself has been stored on a sensory basis without being fully inhabited (Van Der Kolk, 2014). The various and multiple meanings of the experience and its effect on consciousness remain outside awareness only penetrating the survivors' life in unhelpful ways for integration. Psychoanalytic training with a developmental trauma-informed lens may make inhabitation of unexperienced-experience more possible, and the vehicle by which this is made possible is enactment. "Attuning ourselves to the phenomenon of enactment suggests an emerging participatory awareness [but] . . . enactive process is by no means restricted to the therapeutic situation" (Brown, 2020, p. 76). This means the opportunity to engage our thinking and feeling exists in our classrooms, on our training committees, at our conferences, and in our daily lives. We might take up this question regarding the "health" of our inter-systemic self-system and its relationship to peer experience.

Conclusion

It is an uncanny experience to mourn an ambiguous loss over the course of your life. This presence of absence within the survivor sibling experience is transmitted to the next generation. I think the best thing we can hope for is that these experiences get transmitted in ways that are less dissociative and that exist more in verbalization and space between parent and child, teacher and student, and, in multi-sibling families, across the siblings themselves. Inhabiting loss enlivens creative potentialities. On a macro-level, I think it gets expressed when we make room in our psychoanalytic curriculums for the role of peer influence and (dis)/connection, when we train analysts to listen for and encounter lateral relations within the treatment and in our institutes, and when we encourage lateral intimacies and notice how their unravellings affect the individual and collective health of our shared relational worlds. In other words, it's the degree of dissociation and absence of a meditated inhabitation that informs whether the experience is an unnamed shadow or a chapter on love, loss, and family life, that is inherited by the next generation.

This is where the motivation for writing this book comes through. If we can train analysts to consider working through lateral losses and gains, if we can support the unearthing of these kinds of experiences, let them take shape transferentially and counter-transferentially in our offices and within our psychoanalytic institutes, alongside parental and authoritative relations, we do a service for the next generation. We maintain what Apprey (2017) calls "analytic readiness to receive the phantoms of transgenerational haunting when they return" (p. 16). When we open up the possibility of mourning, which allows for new experience to be felt at the time it actually happens, we disrupt a traumatogenic framework from operating across space and time and inhibiting our capacity to feel and to think through lateral experience. We install resiliency and move from survivors to inheritors of a rich experience.

As I was completing this manuscript for the initial submission of this book, I had the following dream:

I was coming home to the building where I now live with my 3 and 1/2 year old son and, to my surprise, my (disabled) brother Teddy was parked out front in his wheelchair. I wonder how he was able to get here by himself as I don't see any aides or accessible vans in sight. He has never visited me on his own, so there is a small thrill that this is possible. As my son and I approach him together, I notice Teddy has a small "voice box" contraption on his wheelchair tray table. Beside him now, my son reaches for the box and enthusiastically fiddles with it, while saying to me, "because of technological advancements, Teddy can now talk!" I'm elated that it might be true but also worried that I just wrote an entire book in which his lack of verbalization and reciprocal participation becomes a defining feature of my psyche. As my son fiddles with the voice box, it soon becomes clear that even this advanced technology cannot change my brother's condition. The contraption doesn't work – no intelligible dialogue can be heard. My son and I are left intuiting what Teddy feels rather than hearing from him directly.

I have had many dreams of my brother Teddy, but never one in which he shows up in my world. I have many associations to this dream, not the least of which is how precociously verbal my toddler appears. I realize that his vocabulary in real-life mimics the dream state and is actually off the charts for his age. Perhaps my longing to connect in this way predisposed my son to become very verbal at an early age. The feeling with which we both approach my brother – my son's excitement and openness to possibility, and my excitement muted by the realities of his restrictions (e.g., how did he get here? Can he suddenly go places of his own volition? Did I dream up my entire childhood? Am I crazy? Was I wrong?) – are in contrast to one another. But that contrast is a comfort: If the next generation can approach the loss without an impaired sense of self or hope, it leaves me feeling hopeful I am not passing this onto my son. The dream to me lays bare the experience I have of longing for my brother. A brother

I would never have dreamed up in a million years, showing up in my life with enough of the reality to not be fantastical (e.g., wheelchair bound) and yet somehow this does not negate the possibility of his active presence. I feel real in this dream; I see my brother too as he is, and my son's willingness to engage across difference, uninhibited in his expression of self. From a self-state perspective, there is more than one "I" represented by the different representations in this dream. I may bring my voicelessness and limited mobility, my presence, my hopefulness, and my grief about what cannot be changed all together into one scene of engagement. This experience is characterized by surprise, which Stern (1990) reminds us, is the affect that often accompanies moving unformulated experience into the realm of the tangible. When we heal the individual wounds within survivor sibling's relational psychic structure left by this early autobiographical experience as well as the attending inherited Big Histories, we necessarily alter what is possible on the collective.

References

Apprey, M. (2017). Representing, theorizing and reconfiguring the concept of transgenerational haunting in order to facilitate healing. In S. Grand & J. Salberg (Eds.), *Transgenerational trauma and the other*. Routledge.

Aron, L. (2018). Beyond tolerance in psychoanalytic communities: Reflexive skepticism and critical pluralism. In L. Aron, S. Grand, & J. Slochower (Eds.), *Decentering relational theory: A comparative critique*. Routledge.

Berman, E. (2004). *Impossible training: A relational view of psychoanalytic education*. The Analytic Press.

Boss, P. (1999). *Ambiguous loss: Learning to live with unresolved grief*. Harvard University Press.

Brown, R. (2020). *Groundwork for a transpersonal psychoanalysis: Spirituality, relationship, and participation*. Routledge.

Clough, P. T. (2013). Intimacy, lateral relationships and biopolitical governance. In A. Frank, P T. Clough, & S. Seidman (Eds.), *Intimacies: A new world of relational life* (pp. 165–180).Routledge.

Cornell, W. (2013). Lost and found: Sibling loss, disconnection, mourning and intimacy. In A. Frank, P. T. Clough, & S. Seidman (Eds.), *Intimacies: A new world of relational life* (pp. 130–145). Routledge.

Dobrich, J. (2020). An elegy for motherless daughters: mourning, dissociation & multiplicity. *Psychoanalytic Perspectives, 17*(3). 366–384.

Gerson, S. (2009). When the third is dead: Memory, mourning & witnessing in the aftermath of the holocaust. *International Journal of Psychoanalysis, 90*, 1341–1357.

Grand, S. (2000). *The reproduction of evil: A clinical and cultural perspective*. The Analytic Press.

Grand, S. (2018). Trauma as radical inquiry. In L. Aron, S. Grand, & J. Slochower (Eds.), *Decentering relational theory: A comparative critique*. Routledge.

Grand, S., & Salberg, J. (2017a). *Trans-generational trauma and the other: Dialogues across history & difference*. Routledge.

Grand, S., & Salberg, J. (Eds.). (2017b). *Wounds of history: Repair and resilience in the transgenerational transmission of trauma*. Routledge.

Harris, A., Roth, M. S., Drescher, J., Butler, D. G., Kirsner, D., & Trosie, D. (2016). Ghosts in psychoanalysis: A crucial counterfeit. In A. Harris, M. Kalb, & S. Klebanoff (Eds.), *Ghosts in the consulting room* (pp. 115–138). Routledge.

Mitchell, J. (2000). *Madmen and medusas: Reclaiming hysteria*. Basic Books.

Mitchell, J. (2003). *Siblings: Sex & violence*. Polity Press.

Ogden, T. (1989). *The primitive edge of experience*. The Analytic Press.

Safer, J. (2002). *The normal one: Life with a difficult or damaged sibling*. The Free Press.

Siegel, D. (1999). *The developing mind: How relationships and the brain interact to shape who we are*. Guilford Press.

Stein, L. (2019). *Working with mystical experiences in psychoanalysis: Opening to the numinous*. Routledge.

Stern, D. B. (1990). Courting surprise: Unbidden experience in clinical practice. *Contemporary Psychoanalysis, 26*, 452–478.

Van Der Kolk, B. (2014). *The body keeps the score: Brain, mind and body in the healing of trauma*. Penguin Group.

Afterword
Sibling self-found

Encountering unexperienced-experience and bearing a capacity to associate and find meaning is not a linear process with a fixed destination.
The words in these pages came together to form particular patterns that
would *undoubtedly* have taken other shapes if written at a different time or
through a different subject. It is the process of *becoming* a subject who can
make meaning of their experience that I hope this collection of personal
stories and interviews illuminates. The meanings that get attributed to the
events themselves are always under revision and indeterminate in nature,
but the capacity to make meaning is often what is hijacked for survivors
of developmental trauma. What made my Mother's storytelling so charged
for me in childhood was that our characters remained fixed. *Who we were*
was a constant. The fiction of being in a steady state was received as an
injunction that foreclosed space for thinking, experiencing, and relating
outside of character – and I hope this book opens up space for others who
may be similarly tasked with maintaining foreclosures, especially in the
realm of siblinghood.

The task of development, as I understand it, is *to become a subject,
among other subjects*. A subject filled with interpellations and objects
that threaten to lead to objectification of the self, the other, and the
world (Guralnik & Simeon, 2010). Subjectivity is a struggle to repeatedly be present to what is, including remembering, experiencing, and
recognizing others as subjects too. Facing reality as a subject is an
unwieldy process that is life long, for all of us. The presence of disability in a sibling does not inherently disrupt development for the survivor
sibling. But inability to mourn the unexpected often creates a series of

adaptations and pathologies within the family that may disable the project of deepening subjectivity. To reclaim one's capacity to seek meaning is to become an embodied subject.

Reference

Guralnik, O., & Simeon, D. (2010). Depersonalization: Standing in the spaces between recognition and interpellation. *Psychoanalytic Dialogues*, *20*(4), 400–416.

Index

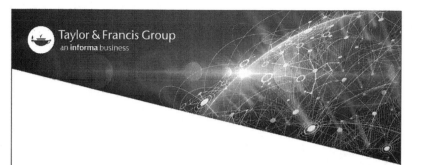